D1188017

Only
Connect

TH FFCL QZ BK

Only Connect

TH FFCL QZ BK

JACK WALEY-COHEN
WITH DAVID MCGAUGHEY

Introductions by
Victoria Coren Mitchell

5 7 9 10 8 6 4

BBC Books, an imprint of Ebury Publishing
20 Vauxhall Bridge Road,
London SW1V 2SA

BBC Books is part of the Penguin Random House group of
companies whose addresses can be found at
global.penguinrandomhouse.com

Text and design copyright © Woodlands Books 2017

Jack Waley-Cohen and David McGaughey have
asserted their right to be identified as the authors of
this Work in accordance with the Copyright,
Designs and Patents Act 1988

This book is published to accompany the television series
entitled *Only Connect* first broadcast on BBC Four in 2008

First published by BBC Books in 2017

www.eburypublishing.co.uk

A CIP catalogue record for this book is available
from the British Library

ISBN 9781785942839

Printed and bound by Clays

Penguin Random House is committed to a sustainable
future for our business, our readers and our planet.
This book is made from Forest Stewardship
Council® certified paper.

CONTENTS

All images © PA Images, except:
pp. 71 (1), 85 (2, 3, 4), 93 (3), 127 (3), 131 (2), 132 (4), 173 (3),
223 (1, 3, 4), 431 (1), 437 (1, 2, 3) © Getty Images
pp. 53 (3, 4), 57 (1, 2), 162 (4) © BBC
pp. 2, 116, 228, 310 © Patrick Olner,
Tall and Short Photography

INTRODUCTION

by Victoria Coren Mitchell

So, how did I come to be standing on a TV set in a spangly frock, helpless and shuddering with giggles, in front of two-and-a-half million viewers, while three highly intelligent, highly respectable civil servants said:

'Malik, Tomlinson, Horan, Payne ... Malik, Tomlinson, Horan, Payne ... Are they golfers?'

Well, it all started with poker. Like everything.

Poker is a beautiful, fiendish, infuriating, irresistible, exasperating and unforgettable game. If poker were a woman, it would be Elizabeth Taylor – and Richard Burton would marry it and divorce it 14 times.

I was beckoned by the poker siren at a young age. I never escaped her clutches, and that is how I came to appear around a smoky baize table in the early, low-budget, ground-breaking TV series *Late Night Poker*, made by an innovative and brilliant Welsh production company.

That is how I came to play in every series of *Late Night Poker* until I became a poker commentator and then a presenter.

And *that* is how I came to be on the other end of the phone when the people from the innovative and brilliant Welsh production company said: 'We've got an idea for a quiz ...'

●　●　●

You know the connection, don't you? Malik, Tomlinson, Horan, Payne?

The beauty of *Only Connect* is that it could always be anything. Highbrow, lowbrow, sidebrow, underbrow. They might be Nobel prize-winning physicists. They might play for Nottingham Forest. They might all rhyme with parts of the body or be French. Perhaps they all mothered illegitimate dukes, or were accused of being Jack the Ripper, or perhaps – if you read their names backwards – they're all types of cheese.

The key is lateral thinking. Can you find those hidden connections in the deepest recesses of your mind, the dustiest corners of your memory? I know, I know: it's hard enough to remember your uncle's name when you bump into him at the supermarket. But on a good day, in a shining lightbulb moment, your brain will deliver to you – triumphantly – the link you're looking for.

Malik, Tomlinson, Horan, Payne … If you don't know the answer, then I'm not going to tell you.

But they are not golfers.

• • •

So, Presentable Productions of Llandaff, Cardiff (now Parasol Media – don't ask me why, but only two more name changes and we've got ourselves a Round 2 question) had an idea for a quiz and they asked if I would host a 'non-broadcast pilot' – a run-through of the format – to show the BBC in the hope of getting it commissioned as a series.

'Fine,' I snitted, 'but only as a special favour to you. If you get the series, you'll have to find someone else to present it. I am an extremely serious and important writer and poker player. I would make a terrible quiz-show host.'

They took what they could get. They only knew poker players, and they guessed I'd be a better host than Black Jack McGraw, the Polish pawnbroker with eight 'missing' business partners. Or, if not *better* than Jack, at least less likely to be in prison at time of recording.

So, we recorded the pilot, a series was commissioned and I found myself unable to back out after all. My heart was lost. I'd fallen head over heels for *Only Connect*. I wouldn't have gone so far down the poker road if I didn't have an addictive personality, and this was an utterly addictive quiz.

Simple enough idea: what is the connection between four apparently random clues? But this is a very tough quiz. The link can be very difficult to spot. (The comedian Mark Steel once tweeted, 'I love Only Connect, with its answers like "They're all anagrams of Swedish slang words for pomegranate."') Or, as in the case of Malik, Horan, Tomlinson and Payne, it can be – theoretically – easy to spot. Either way, the connection is there.

Then, on to Round 2, where we up the ante by asking not only what is the connection but *what comes next in a sequence*.

Round 3: up it again by demanding *four connections simultaneously*, on a fiendish 'connecting wall' with 16 jumbled-up clues, featuring red herrings that fit into more than one category but only one possible complete solution.

Round 4: nothing to do with the rest of the quiz. The 'Missing Vowels' round. You have to work out what are the well-known names or phrases from which the vowels have been removed and the consonants re-spaced. The round simply isn't about connections. Nobody knows why it's there. Then again, the same is true of me.

Well, now you know why I'm there. They didn't know who else to ask, and I was too hooked by the format to walk away. But my original instinct was right: I am a terrible quiz-show host.

Good quiz-show hosts are irrepressibly cheery, full of bounce and vigour, with an enormous natural warmth. I am socially awkward, physically lazy and constantly irritable with hunger. I always want to be sitting down; I'm too short-sighted to read an autocue, yet too squeamish for contact lenses and too vain for glasses, so I stare into space, blinking like a cartoon scapegoat, trying to remember what I'd meant to say next.

'*Only Connect* is back!' cheered the *Radio Times* (always a great supporter of ours) in about 2012. 'And Victoria's in the chair with her trademark withering glare!'

That was supposed to be my welcoming smile.

• • •

Luckily, somehow, as if by magic, my peculiarities turned out to suit the quiz. It's a peculiar quiz.

If this were an episode of *Only Connect*, I would now add: 'And God knows we have peculiar contestants!'

I don't really think they're peculiar. I just enjoy making jokes about the fact that they might *seem* peculiar, relative to the prejudices of modern television. I actually identify with them very closely.

I think of myself as a 'geek': short-sighted, prone to hay fever, riddled with tics and compulsions, fundamentally uninterested in fashion, highly likely to be the last one picked for a sports team. Luckily, the day I left school I opted out of a value system that considers these traits to be 'failings'. I'm proud of my arcane interests, quirky hobbies and healthy suspicion of consensus.

I imagine the *Only Connect* family as a community of those who shivered on the edges of the school playground, furiously underestimated by meat-heads with the wrong priorities.

Of course, some of our contestants are perfectly cool in a straightforward way: good-looking, articulate and confident. Nevertheless, I like to celebrate the geek soul in all of us. We are the sitters and readers, the studiers and stamp-collectors, the museum visitors and chamber music players, the coders and counters, the speakers of ancient languages and historic battle re-enactors. (Another tweet of Mark Steel's: 'The first contestant on Only Connect tonight built a lifesize model of Von Ribbentrop out of earwigs.')

Increasingly, as time has gone on, I've characterised us as weedy and awkward, unconventional and stubborn, pale, myopic and wheezy. The programme itself, I once explained to viewers, has a nervous disorder and wears orthopaedic shoes. Another time, I revealed that *Only Connect* has been questioned over the disappearance of several missing hitch-hikers.

Naturally, in the classic British tradition, this is all highly celebratory. There is no better way to express love, pride and comradeship than by mickey-taking. My real satirical target, I hope it has always been clear, is the mainstream.

This was easy because *Only Connect* never *was* mainstream. We were made for BBC Four, a cultish, non-terrestrial channel for an eager, curious audience. We were there to entertain the sort of viewer who might run screaming from *The X Factor* into the comforting arms of a documentary about biplanes or molecular biology. Not a viewer who necessarily *knew* about these things, but who was *interested* to know about anything. I hope we kept that cultish flavour as we stumbled, blinking and nervous, into the bright lights of BBC Two.

The way we identify our questions, for example, is highly rarefied. They're separated into

LION
WATER
TWO REEDS
TWISTED FLAX
HORNED VIPER
and
EYE OF HORUS.

Why? Well, for the first three series they were identified by Greek letters – alpha, beta, gamma and

INTRODUCTION

so on. Although the BBC Four viewers fell quickly in love with the essential connecting principles of the quiz, we had a lot of complaints about the Greek letters. People considered it a pretentious gimmick. The complaints built and built. The letters had to go. On the other hand, I hate to give in to peer pressure.

There was only one thing for it. At the beginning of the fourth series, inspired by a cartoon that a good-natured fellow called @frizfrizzle had posted on Twitter, I said something like:

'Many people have complained about our board of Greek letters. They say it's exclusive, pretentious, snooty and smug. Never let it be said the BBC fails to listen to its audience! We've listened! The Greek letters have gone. So, Epicureans, please choose ... your Egyptian hieroglyph!'

That was really the beginning of the show starting to take the mickey out of itself. I think it was a happy direction. From then on, we found our identity: a show that both venerates arcane knowledge and finds a veneration for arcane knowledge mildly ridiculous.

Most of the quizzers on *Only Connect* are a lot cleverer than I am. But we share a mindset; we understand each other. The same is true of the viewers – even those who never get any of the answers and tune in for the sheer pleasure of watching people who can. Those viewers watch the final stages, as I do myself, in the same spirit as you'd watch Roger Federer or Serena Williams playing at Wimbledon: in awe at the gymnastics, dazzled by the ability, delighted to watch a fellow human at the peak of their powers.

And yet, it feels appropriate to tease them throughout. I don't know why. In *I'm Sorry I Haven't a Clue* (a radio series that our long-term viewers will know I revere), the great Humphrey Lyttelton relished opportunities to make remarks at the panellists' expense. His magnificent successor Jack Dee has taken up that baton with glee. When I do the same with our contestants, I mean it both as an homage to that wonderful radio show and a sign that I think of the teams as friends and colleagues – just as those great professional radio performers do each other.

'Welcome to our cookery special,' I said in a recent episode. 'Tonight, in the style of *The Great British Bake Off*, we'll be featuring a signature dish, a technical challenge and a show-stopping fruitcake. I'll let you decide who's who as we meet the teams.'

Another week, I said: 'If you're worried that your house might be haunted by a ghost and needs exorcising, there's a very simple way to work out whether it is or it isn't: it isn't. But speaking of having a fright, let's meet the teams.'

I hope they don't mind. I hope they hear the echo of *I'm Sorry I Haven't a Clue*, and the love and kinship. I think they do. The one thing people always say, when they've come along to Cardiff and taken part in the quiz, is how friendly and warm it all is. Almost everyone on the crew is Welsh, most of the people in charge are women, and I honestly believe it might be the nicest, kindest production in the world.

After the last series, Jenny the producer gave all the finalists a bag of Welsh cakes to take home. Her mother had been up all night baking them.

I don't think that happened on *The Krypton Factor*.

· · ·

In this book, you will find some of the best questions from the first ten broadcast series of *Only Connect*, as selected by our question editors Jack Waley-Cohen and David McGaughey, plus some brand-new (never broadcast) Connecting Walls and Missing Vowels rounds.

Jack and David are new to the job of question editor, though not to *Only Connect* – Jack's quiz team got to the final of our very first series, back in 2008, when I wore scratchy beige trouser suits and didn't make any jokes. (*And the programme was all the better for it*, no doubt some viewers would sniff.)

So, you may have seen some of these questions before. If you have never missed an episode of *Only Connect* then you will have seen *many* of these questions before. Will it make any difference to your scores? I'd be interested to know. Me, I get a lot of questions wrong when I watch episodes of

Only Connect go out on TV, and I was there when we recorded them!

Somehow, because the essence of the challenge is lateral thinking rather than knowledge, I can be bamboozled by them two or three times over. You might be told where Battle Abbey is and never need to be told again, but you wouldn't necessarily remember what that has in common with the champion of the 1981 Grand National. And if you can't work it out, you will find two more clues and the answer in a few pages' time ...

You will also find the connecting wall that features Malik, Tomlinson, Horan and Payne. Good luck with that one.

They didn't all play for Nottingham Forest.

CONNECTIONS

CONNECTIONS

There are various ways to 'use' this book. It's divided into four sections: Round 1 'Connections'; Round 2 'Sequences', Round 3 'Connecting Walls' and Round 4 'Missing Vowels'. Then there is an audition paper at the back.

You can read it/play it at random. Flick through, take questions from anywhere, see how you get on.

If you want to control the difficulty level, bear in mind that the questions get progressively more difficult throughout each section.

This mimics the series itself. Every time a new series starts, viewers cry: 'It's got easier! It's been dumbed down!' That's because they last saw it a few months or a year before, during the last and most difficult stages of the previous series. Now, it returns with the opening heats, which are always less hard. It's a false comparison.

I usually know when an episode is correctly pitched. Some weeks before we go into production, I receive a huge secret parcel full of question packs for the upcoming series. I then play them all, as if I were a team. What should happen is that I score reasonably highly during the opening heats. My score starts to even out in the middle of the series. By the quarter-finals, I am getting low scores. By the semi-finals, I'm scoring practically nothing. By the final, I don't even understand the questions.

If you prefer to 'play' this book in a more rigid and formalised way – and frankly, I'd be disappointed in our fans if none of you did – then you will find, if you look deeper, that they can be separated into complete *Only Connect* games.

So, you could play your way through a set of six Round 1 questions, going through the hieroglyphs from Two Reeds to Eye of Horus, then jump to the 'matching' set of six Round 2 questions (and the same hieroglyphs).

The first six questions of Round 1 will be of equivalent difficulty to the first six of Round 2, and so on. Each set has two connecting walls (Lion and Water) and four sets of missing vowels (Two Reeds, Twisted Flax, Horned Viper and Eye of Horus) of equivalent difficulty.

By separating the sections into sets of 6–6–2–4 in this way, you can play out episode-length games of *Only Connect* – alone or with a group of friends for a party.

Of course, you're the type of person who buys the *Only Connect* book. So it's probably alone.

• • • •

We kick off with Round 1: what is the connection between four apparently random clues?

'Connections' is the defining round of the quiz, the main thing that people talk about when they explain what *Only Connect* is. Finding the hidden connection between random things has a deep satisfaction to it. There's something very pleasing, especially to us OC-types with our chaotic, anxious brains, about putting things in groups: sorting, solving, categorising, connecting. It's what we love about Sherlock Holmes stories, about crosswords, about maths. It's what I love about poker. For a moment, you can make the world seem ordered and rational.

But you don't have to be a geek to love spotting connections. For example, my mother-in-law, a supremely natural, communicative, happy and well-adjusted woman, loves to hear that this person's neighbour is that person's cousin. Or this person's boss is that person's daughter. She is pleased and comforted to see the web of the world laid bare.

I've never met anyone who wasn't tickled to discover that Fred Trueman's daughter married Raquel Welch's son. Or that the comic Tom O'Connor is the father-in-law of the athlete Denise Lewis. Everyone has a taste for that six-degrees-of-Kevin-Bacon.

From there, it's just a short hop to wondering what connects Switzerland and a photon; Danny Boyle and Winston Churchill; Roquefort cheese and the Dead Sea Scrolls. (All of these are to be found in the forthcoming pages of the first section.)

Connections make the world feel smaller and safer – more claustrophobic, perhaps, but more controlled for that. The challenge for our question writers is to keep looking harder and further, deeper and wider, for those hidden, pleasing links.

On the show, the fewer Round 1 clues you need to see before naming the connection, the more points you can get.

Five points are available for getting it after just one clue (which is difficult, and involves a willingness to gamble, but crucially – on the right sort of question – not impossible).

Three points if you've seen two clues, two points after three clues and one point if you've seen all four. (It's also one point to the opposing team if the question is 'thrown over for a bonus'.)

Obviously, you can recreate this experience by covering up the clues with a bit of paper and revealing them to yourself gradually. Or by asking the question master to read them out one by one, pausing after each and not continuing until you shout, 'Next!'

(I say 'question master'. I know it's just you in a different voice. Running back and forth across the room.)

I'm now going to leave you with Jack and David for the questions. I'll see you at Round 2!

VCM

5 points

Reunion of
broken parts

3 points

Pebble

2 points

Measurement
of the Earth

1 point

Triangle
measurement

| Reunion of broken parts | Pebble | Measurement of the Earth | Triangle measurement |

Meanings or derivations of mathematical disciplines

- Algebra – from Arabic
- Calculus – from Latin. A calculus was a small pebble for counting on an abacus.
- Geometry – from Ancient Greek
- Trigonometry – also from Ancient Greek

This question stumped the Lapsed Psychologists in the final of the first series, allowing the Crossworders to pick up a bonus point on their way to becoming champions.

5 points

3 points

2 points

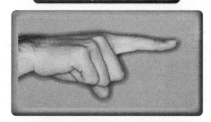

1 point

Parts of a book

- Appendix
- Spine
- Index (finger)
- Page (boys)

The Gallifreyans scored 3 points on this question. After Clue 1 they were tempted to guess and were kicking themselves after seeing Clue 2, when they realised they could have had 5 points.

It takes luck, knowledge, skill and bravery to score 5 points on a Round 1 question. It wasn't until the 47th episode that it happened for the first time, when Chris Quinn of the Alesmen knew about Pugachev's Cobra.

5 points

Incognito

3 points

Unbeknownst

2 points

Nonchalant

1 point

Misnomer

| Incognito | Unbeknownst | Nonchalant | Misnomer |

Words that have no 'positive' opposite

- Incognito: there is no 'cognito'.
- Unbeknownst: there is no 'beknownst'.
- Nonchalant: there is no 'chalant'.
- Misnomer: there is no 'nomer'.

Neither team scored on this question from series 7. The Science Editors guessed 'loan words from French', and the Board Gamers (who went on to win the series) offered 'start with negative prefixes' – which is true, but it missed the point.

5 points

Islamic Emirate
of Afghanistan

3 points

Cornwall

2 points

Pirate ship

1 point

Finish of a
motor race

| Islamic Emirate of Afghanistan | Cornwall | Pirate ship | Finish of a motor race |

Black-and-white flags

- The flag of the Taliban was also the flag of Afghanistan from 1997 to 2001.
- St Piran's Flag is the flag of Cornwall.
- The Jolly Roger, or Skull and Crossbones, was hoisted on eighteenth-century pirate ships.
- A chequered black-and-white flag is waved as the winner and subsequent finishers of a motor race cross the line.

The Bakers scored 2 points on this after toying with 'places that wanted independence'. The flag of Afghanistan is now black, red and green with the country's emblem at its centre.

5 points

Sunset Boulevard

3 points

American Beauty

2 points

The Lovely Bones

1 point

Desperate Housewives

Sunset Boulevard	American Beauty	The Lovely Bones	Desperate Housewives

Narrated by dead people

- *Sunset Boulevard* is narrated by Joe Gillis, found lying face down in the swimming pool.
- Lester Burnham opens the film *American Beauty* with the words: 'In less than a year, I will be dead.'
- Fourteen-year-old Susie Salmon narrates Alice Sebold's *The Lovely Bones* from heaven.
- Mary Alice Young blows her own head off at the start of season 1 of *Desperate Housewives*.

The street where the Burnhams live in *American Beauty* is called Robin Hood Trail.

A rare example of a question that stumped the mighty Crossworders: they guessed 'large age-gap relationships' after seeing *The Lovely Bones* – before the Edinburgh Scrabblers picked up a bonus point.

5 points

Manufacturing gunpowder

3 points

Roman mouthwash

2 points

Thickening wool

1 point

Marking territory

| Manufacturing gunpowder | Roman mouthwash | Thickening wool | Marking territory |

Uses for urine

- Urine contains a high amount of ammonia, which can be used in gunpowder.
- Urine was used in mouthwash and toothpaste until the eighteenth century.
- A fuller would use urine to clean and thicken cloth. It was then hung 'on tenterhooks' to dry, hence the phrase.
- Marking territory with urine is performed by various animals to spread their pheromones.

Urine imported from Portugal was especially popular as mouthwash in Roman times because it was said to have been the strongest in Europe.

This question is a good example of the show's classic 'four apparently random clues', which, finally, by Clue 4, no longer seem random at all. The Educators scored 1 point on this after seeing all four clues.

5 points

Ionising radiation

3 points

People in *Brave New World*

2 points

Stars in a constellation

1 point

Only Connect questions (series 1-3)

| Ionising radiation | People in *Brave New World* | Stars in a constellation | *Only Connect* questions (series 1–3) |

Labelled by Greek letters

- Ionising radiation has three types called alpha, beta and gamma.
- In Aldous Huxley's *Brave New World*, society is split into castes called Alphas, Betas, Gammas, Deltas and Epsilons.
- Stars are labelled by Bayer letters. Usually, alpha is the brightest star, beta the next brightest, etc.
- Greek letters were used for the first three series of *Only Connect*, before switching to the Egyptian Hieroglyphs you now know and love.

In series 2 (yes, we've edited Clue 4), the Chessmen were onto it from Clue 1, considered gambling after Clue 2, but played it safe and took the third clue before confirming the answer.

5 points

3 points

2 points

1 point

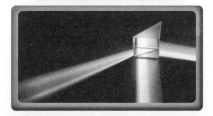

Depicted on Pink Floyd album covers

- Battersea Power Station: *Animals* (1977)
- Handshake: *Wish You Were Here* (1975)
- Wall: *The Wall* (1979)
- Prism: *The Dark Side of the Moon* (1973)

It's quite unusual for an *Only Connect* picture question actually to be about pictures! Other potential clues could have been 'A cow' for the album *Atom Heart Mother*, and 'Pink Floyd' for *The Piper at the Gates of Dawn*. These images are, of course, not the actual images used on the album covers – that would probably be too easy!

The Fell Walkers scored 2 points on this series 7 question.

5 points

Büsingen:
Switzerland

3 points

Monaco:
France

2 points

Berwick:
Scotland

1 point

Swansea:
England

Büsingen: Switzerland	Monaco: France	Berwick: Scotland	Swansea: England

Football clubs playing in a non-native league

- FC Büsingen: German side playing in Switzerland
- AS Monaco: Monegasque side playing in France
- Berwick Rangers: English side playing in Scotland
- Swansea City: Welsh side playing in England

Chester FC (the successor club to the liquidated Chester City) plays in the English league but (according to many maps) has a stadium that is partly in England and partly in Wales.

No points here for the Globetrotters, and the Board Gamers didn't pick up the bonus either.

5 points

Ladybird:
yellow

3 points

Cockroach:
colourless

2 points

Spock:
green

1 point

You:
red

25

Ladybird: yellow	Cockroach: colourless	Spock: green	You: red

Blood colour

- Ladybirds secrete yellow blood to ward off predators.
- A cockroach's blood is colourless because it contains no haemoglobin.
- Spock has green blood because of the copper in it.
- You have red blood.

In situations where the vital fluid doesn't contain red blood cells, it should be called 'lymph', technically.

As was famously said by Clive Tyldesley of Liverpool FC stalwart Jamie Carragher: 'If you cut him open, he'll bleed red.'

The Cinephiles were onto this quickly, though they thought ladybirds had green blood. Spock confirmed the answer for them and they scored 2 points.

5 points

Australian gold

3 points

Antiguan and Barbudan silver

2 points

Portuguese platinum

1 point

Cuban copper

| Australian gold | Antiguan and Barbudan silver | Portuguese platinum | Cuban copper |

Matching web country codes and chemical symbols

- .au is Australia's top-level domain name. Au is the symbol for gold.
- .ag is Antigua and Barbuda's top-level domain name. Ag is the symbol for silver.
- .pt is Portugal's top-level domain name. Pt is the symbol for platinum.
- .cu is Cuba's top-level domain name. Cu is the symbol for copper.

Australia's earliest top-level domain name was .oz. The .oz websites were reassigned to .oz.au when .au became official.

1 point for the Nightwatchmen. After Clue 2 they thought it was something to do with ships, before fumbling their way to the point in the end.

5 points

Absolutely anybody

3 points

Male leads in *3rd Rock from the Sun*

2 points

Tunnels in *The Great Escape*

1 point

Presidents Jefferson, Nixon and Truman

29

Absolutely anybody	Male leads in *3rd Rock from the Sun*	Tunnels in *The Great Escape*	Presidents Jefferson, Nixon and Truman

Tom, Dick and Harry

- Absolutely anybody is 'any old Tom, Dick and Harry'.
- In *3rd Rock from the Sun*, Tom(my), Dick and Harry Solomon are aliens who come to Earth to learn its customs.
- The tunnel called Tom was discovered by the Germans in *The Great Escape*. Harry was the tunnel ultimately used for the escape.
- US Presidents Thomas Jefferson, Richard Nixon and Harry S. Truman.

The Oenophiles knew it as soon as they saw *The Great Escape* clue. It isn't always the hardest clue that comes first: here, 'Absolutely anybody' is possibly the easiest clue, but that doesn't make it the most obvious.

5 points

Wee

3 points

Unhyphenated

2 points

Penultimate

1 point

Pentasyllabic

| Wee | Unhyphenated | Penultimate | Pentasyllabic |

Autological words

These words all describe themselves

- Wee: word meaning tiny, which itself is tiny, having only three letters.
- Unhyphenated: word meaning without a hyphen, which is itself unhyphenated.
- Penultimate: word meaning one before last, which it is, in this specific context of four clues.
- Pentasyllabic: word meaning 'consisting of five syllables', which has five syllables.

No points for either team in this puzzler. The Record Collectors couldn't think of a guess, and the Welsh Learners were inspired by 'Wee' and guessed 'Games consoles'.

5 points

2nd female
Nobel laureate
in science

3 points

Leader of
2nd Labour
government

2 points

2nd Super Bowl
winners

1 point

2nd rule of
Fight Club

ANSWERS

2nd female Nobel laureate in science	Leader of 2nd Labour government	2nd Super Bowl winners	2nd rule of Fight Club

Same as the first

- Marie Skłodowska Curie shared the Nobel prize for Physics in 1903, and won the Nobel prize for Chemistry in 1911.
- James Ramsay MacDonald led the first ever Labour government briefly in 1924, and again in 1929, following Stanley Baldwin's second premiership.
- The Green Bay Packers won Super Bowl I vs the Kansas City Chiefs in 1967, and Super Bowl II vs the Oakland Raiders in 1968.
- Both the first two rules of Fight Club are 'You do not talk about Fight Club'. The 1999 film directed by David Fincher was based on a 1996 novel by Chuck Palahniuk.

The Bakers scored 3 points here on their way to victory over the Globetrotters.

5 points

Mr Fusion

3 points

Dehydrated pizza

2 points

Self-tying shoes

1 point

Hoverboard

| Mr Fusion | Dehydrated pizza | Self-tying shoes | Hoverboard |

Back to the Future's 2015

- Mr Fusion is a home nuclear fusion reactor that runs on household rubbish.
- Pizza is rehydrated before eating.
- Self-tying shoes lace up themselves.
- A hoverboard is a hovering skateboard.

Among other outlandish predictions, there was *Jaws 19* and a female president of the USA.

The self-tying shoes did it for the Politicos as they picked up 2 points.

5 points

Welsh
RH, NG

3 points

French
K, W, X, Y, Z

2 points

German
Q, Y

1 point

English
Q, Z

Welsh RH, NG	French K, W, X, Y, Z	German Q, Y	English Q, Z

10 points in Scrabble

- Each of the letters is worth 10 points in that language's version of Scrabble.

Welsh Scrabble has no Q, X or Z but has various double letter tiles (digraphs, for example dd = 1). It is not permissible to use the individual letters to spell these out.

This is a good example of a question where you only receive a piece of information you're likely actually to know at Clue 4, but on the right day a team might work out what is going on much earlier.

The Cat Lovers realised they were uncommon letters in each language (though their captain had '*Zut alors*' as a counter example for French usage of the letter. Z) and ended up with 1 point.

5 points

3 points

2 points

1 point

First names are national capital cities

- WASHINGTON Irving: American writer of 'Rip Van Winkle' and 'The Legend of Sleepy Hollow'; Washington, DC is the capital of the USA.
- VICTORIA Coren Mitchell: British author, poker player and presenter of *Only Connect*; Victoria is the capital of the Seychelles.
- SOFIA Coppola: American director best known for *Lost in Translation*; Sofia is the capital of Bulgaria.
- PARIS Hilton: American socialite and businesswoman; Paris is the capital of France.

The Chessmen thought the first picture was Walter Scott or Robert Burns, which caused them a little trouble before they picked up 1 point.

5 points

Professor Layton

3 points

Uncle Sam

2 points

Alan Sugar

1 point

Lord Kitchener

| Professor Layton | Uncle Sam | Alan Sugar | Lord Kitchener |

Famous for pointing their finger

- Professor Layton is a puzzle-solving computer-game character who regularly points (e.g. to accuse someone of wrongdoing).
- Uncle Sam pointed on the 'I Want YOU for U.S. Army' posters used in World War I and World War II.
- Alan Sugar points when he fires candidates on *The Apprentice*.
- Lord Kitchener pointed on 'Your Country Needs YOU' recruitment posters for World War I.

Other famous finger-pointers are Malcolm X, Usain Bolt and Alberto Giacometti's sculpture *Pointing Man*, which sold for $141 million in 2015.

1 point for the Analysts (the series 5 champions) with a bit of good guesswork.

5 points

Football
League One

3 points

5ive on
The Big Reunion

2 points

Millipede

1 point

Hundred
Years' War

| Football League One | 5ive on *The Big Reunion* | Millipede | Hundred Years' War |

Misleading numbers

The number within the name is not an accurate representation:

- With the Premier League and the Championship above, Football League One is the third tier of English football.
- J. Brown was missing from 5ive, hence there were four of them.
- Millipedes may have several hundred legs, but never 1,000 as the 'milli' in their name suggests.
- The Hundred Years War lasted from 1337 to 1453, rather more than 100 years.

At various stages 5ive has appeared with 4our or thr3e members.

The Relatives clicked that a millipede doesn't have 1,000 legs, and scored 2 points.

5 points

George V

3 points

Stalingrad

2 points

Victor Hugo

1 point

Concorde

| George V | Stalingrad | Victor Hugo | Concorde |

Paris Métro stations

- George V is named after our own king.
- Stalingrad takes its name from the World War II battle.
- Victor Hugo is named after the French author.
- Concorde Métro station is at the Place de la Concorde.

Other stations include Garibaldi, Franklin D. Roosevelt and Alexandre Dumas.

This was used with slightly different clues as a picture question in the final of series 1 between the Crossworders (who went on to become Champions of Champions of Champions) and the Lapsed Psychologists. The teams identified that there was a connection with France, but couldn't quite pin it down, so no points scored for anyone.

5 points

COOKIE

3 points

CHOC-ICE

2 points

DIOXIDE

1 point

BEDECKED

| COOKIE | CHOC-ICE | DIOXIDE | BEDECKED |

Words with horizontal symmetry

- The bottom half is a mirror image of the top half – any word using only BCDEHIKOX shares this property.

In this question, no clue is necessarily any easier than the next; it's just that the more clues you see, the more likely you are to work it out. Capital letters or unusual spelling or presentation of clues like this in *Only Connect* questions can often indicate a puzzle that extends beyond the meaning of the words.

The Chessmen picked up a bonus point on this question after the Rugby Boys (who went on to win series 2, in no small part due to the contributions of team member Mark Labbett, now a 'Chaser' on the TV quiz *The Chase*) came close without quite pinning down the precise connection.

5 points

Orphans in *Oliver Twist*

3 points

Sue Grafton's detective novel series

2 points

Series of *QI*

1 point

UK storms (since 2015)

| Orphans in *Oliver Twist* | Sue Grafton's detective novel series | Series of *QI* | UK storms (since 2015) |

Labelled in A, B, C … order

- Mr Bumble names the orphans in alphabetical order in *Oliver Twist*. The full quote from the book: 'We name our fondlings in alphabetical order. The last was a S,--Swubble, I named him. This was a T,--Twist, I named *him*. The next one as comes will be Unwin, and the next Vilkins.'
- Sue Grafton's 'Alphabet Series', featuring female private eye Kinsey Millhone, began with *'A' is for Alibi* in 1982.
- Each series of *QI* is labelled A, B, C … and the episodes in each series have titles or themes beginning with that letter. The first series hosted by Sandi Toksvig was the 'N' series.
- In 2015, the UK Storm Centre began naming storms from an alphabetical list, just as tropical storms in the Atlantic have been given names for many years. The first named UK storm was Storm Abigail in November 2015.

The Fell Walkers scored 2 points on this – though we've tweaked the clues and changed the order from the original now that the UK gives names to storms. The original had 'Tropical storms' as Clue 2.

5 points

Crossrail

3 points

169,000 sq. miles of British Antarctica

2 points

Big Ben's Clock Tower

1 point

2012 Olympic Park

| Crossrail | 169,000 sq. miles of British Antarctica | Big Ben's Clock Tower | 2012 Olympic Park |

Renamed in honour of Queen Elizabeth II

- Crossrail, the new West–East railway line (from Reading to Shenfield via central London) is to be known as the Elizabeth Line.
- The southern part of the British Antarctic Territory was named Queen Elizabeth Land in 2012.
- Big Ben's Clock Tower was renamed Elizabeth Tower in 2012.
- The 2012 Olympic Park was renamed Queen Elizabeth Olympic Park when it reopened in 2013.

A version of this question was used in the 2015 Comic Relief special, and earned 3 points for the Water Babies (Reeta Chakrabarti, Tom Holland, Patrick Marber) in their match against the Tillers (Katie Derham, Steve Pemberton, Professor Steve Jones).

5 points

3 points

2 points

1 point

Goldilocks

Goldilocks enters the house of the three bears and eats porridge out of their bowls before sleeping in their beds.

- Flower BEDS
- A game of BOWLS
- The sitcom *PORRIDGE*
- Three pictures of Bear Grylls (THREE BEARS)

The story was first published by Robert Southey; his version has an old hag, rather than Goldilocks, intrude in the bears' home. The story had been doing the rounds for many years before he wrote and published his version in 1837.

The Exhibitionists realised it was Goldilocks, but accidentally said 'Little Red Riding Hood', so it went over for an easy bonus point to the Relatives.

5 points

Byrne vs Fischer, 1956

3 points

Lindbergh baby kidnapping, 1932

2 points

Warne bowls Gatting, Old Trafford, 1993

1 point

'The Quiz of the Week'

| Byrne vs Fischer, 1956 | Lindbergh baby kidnapping, 1932 | Warne bowls Gatting, Old Trafford, 1993 | 'The Quiz of the Week' |

_____ of the Century

- Donald Byrne vs Bobby Fischer was chess's 'Game of the Century'.
- The title 'The Crime of the Century' was given to the Lindbergh baby kidnapping.
- Shane Warne's dismissal of Mike Gatting was cricket's 'Ball of the Century'.
- TV show *Sale of the Century* described itself as 'The Quiz of the Week' at the start of each episode.

Shane Warne's delivery to Mike Gatting, his first ball in Ashes cricket, was celebrated in the song 'Jiggery Pokery' by the Duckworth Lewis Method.

The Crossworders faced this question in their victory against a team of *Mastermind* Champions – and picked up 2 points.

5 points

3 points

2 points

1 point

ANSWERS

Palindromic surnames

- Yoko ONO, artist and wife of John Lennon
- John HANNAH, Scottish actor
- Monica SELES, tennis player
- Trevor EVE, British actor

Tim Smit, who conceived the Eden Project in Cornwall, takes it a step further with his wholly palindromic name.

This question drew a blank for both the Ombudsmen and the County Councillors.

5 points

Shot Al Capone
in the foot

3 points

Crowned
Napoleon I

2 points

Presented Irving
Berlin's Oscar

1 point

Amputated Aron
Ralston's arm

ANSWERS

Shot Al Capone in the foot	Crowned Napoleon I	Presented Irving Berlin's Oscar	Amputated Aron Ralston's arm

Did it themselves

- Al Capone accidentally shot himself in the foot by setting off a revolver in his golf bag as he rummaged for a club.
- In 1804, Napoleon I brought Pope Pius VII to crown him in Notre-Dame cathedral, but seized the crown and crowned himself.
- When presenting the 1942 Academy Award for Best Song, Irving Berlin opened the envelope to find he had won it himself for 'White Christmas'.
- Trapped in a canyon, Aron Ralston cut off his own arm with a multi-tool to escape, as depicted in the Danny Boyle film *127 Hours*.

The Coders guessed 'these people don't exist', and the QI Elves gratefully picked up a bonus point.

5 points

Covert

3 points

creMate

2 points

fEast

1 point

fRiend

| Covert | creMate | fEast | fRiend |

Delete the capital to make an opposite.

- Covert and Overt
- Cremate and Create
- Feast and Fast
- Friend and Fiend

The Cat Lovers realised that new words were created if you removed the capitalised letter, but they couldn't quite pin it down exactly – and the Celts then picked up a bonus point.

5 points

Sierpinski triangle

3 points

The Blind Assassin

2 points

Matryoshka

1 point

Inception

Sierpinski triangle	*The Blind Assassin*	Matryoshka	*Inception*

Make use of recursion

DON'T ACCEPT: anything specific to just one clue, e.g. they're all a dream within a dream

These are all 'things within things'.

- The Sierpinski triangle is a fractal based around repeatedly subdividing triangles into smaller triangles.
- Margaret Atwood's *The Blind Assassin*, published in 2000, is also the title of a book written by a character in the novel, and that book is about a story with the same title again.
- Matryoshka is a name for Russian nesting dolls.
- Characters enter dreams within dreams in the 2010 film *Inception*.

The Numerists were sniffing around the correct answer from Clue 1, and eventually scored 2 points.

5 points

Márquez
the Explorer

3 points

Fireman
Peyton-Jones

2 points

Mouseling
Ballerina

1 point

Postman
Clifton

| Márquez the Explorer | Fireman Peyton-Jones | Mouseling Ballerina | Postman Clifton |

Surnames of children's characters

- *Dora the Explorer*, the American animated show, is centred on Dora Márquez.
- Sam Peyton Jones is the lead character in *Fireman Sam*, the Welsh animated show.
- Angelina Mouseling is the ballerina in *Angelina Ballerina*, the British series.
- Pat Clifton is the eponymous postman in *Postman Pat*.

Fireman Sam lives in Pontypandy, an amalgam of Pontypridd and Tonypandy.

The Software Engineers were getting close, but their guess of 'Rhyming animated characters' didn't hit the mark – and the Erstwhiles took the bonus point.

5 points

Photon

3 points

White corners

2 points

Switzerland

1 point

Gearbox disconnected from transmission

| Photon | White corners | Switzerland | Gearbox disconnected from transmission |

Neutral

- In physics, a photon is a type of particle with no electrical charge.
- White corners of a boxing ring are the neutral corners. When a boxer is knocked down, the opponent has to go to the farthest neutral corner.
- Switzerland is well known for being neutral in various world affairs.
- A car is in neutral when the gearbox is disconnected from transmission.

1 point for the Urban Walkers who went on a bit of a journey with a version of this question before settling on the correct answer.

5 points

Unloose

3 points

Debone

2 points

Irregardless

1 point

Inflammable

| Unloose | Debone | Irregardless | Inflammable |

Same meaning without the prefix

- 'Unloose' means the same as 'loose'.
- 'Bone' means the same as 'debone'.
- 'Irregardless' means the same as 'regardless'.
- 'Inflammable' means the same as 'flammable'.

Other examples are 'unravel' and 'unthaw'.

The Bloggers thought Clue 1 wasn't a real word. After Clue 2, they suggested 'you bone something not debone them', after which they offered the answer 'you can't unloose but you can loose, you can't debone but you can bone', which was wrong. The Wrights then got it right for a bonus point.

5 points

3 points

2 points

1 point

Mean something bad when upside down

- A 'Justice' tarot card upside down indicates unfairness.
- The Union Jack upside down is a sign of distress.
- A horseshoe upside down is unlucky.
- Thumbs down usually registers disapproval.

The Analysts identified all the clues, but only as time ran out did one of them say 'right way up'. The bonus point went to the Antiquarians who knew it anyway.

5 points

Champion of 1981
Grand National

3 points

It tells of
Pennywise
the clown

2 points

Town where
Battle Abbey lies

1 point

Had a 1974 hit
with 'Killer Queen'

| Champion of 1981 Grand National | It tells of Pennywise the clown | Town where Battle Abbey lies | Had a 1974 hit with 'Killer Queen' |

Answer is in the clue

- Bob Champion won the Grand National, riding Aldaniti.
- Pennywise features in the 1986 novel It by Stephen King.
- The abbey is in Battle, East Sussex – not Hastings, which is nearby.
- Queen single 'Killer Queen' reached no. 2 in the UK.

Definitely a chance to score 5 points in this question from the final of series 6, and indeed the Draughtsmen knew about Bob Champion in the 1981 Grand National. However, they lost the thread a little and it went over to the Scribes for a bonus point on their way to becoming series champions.

5 points

Injun Joe's body

3 points

Roquefort cheese

2 points

Dead Sea Scrolls

1 point

Troglodytes

| Injun Joe's body | Roquefort cheese | Dead Sea Scrolls | Troglodytes |

Found in caves

- In *The Adventures of Tom Sawyer*, a dangerous cave is blocked up for safety but Injun Joe is trapped inside and starves to death.
- Roquefort undergoes final ageing in the limestone caves near Toulouse where the atmosphere promotes growth of the mould *Penicillium roqueforti*.
- The Dead Sea Scrolls are the (mostly Hebrew) manuscripts found in caves in the Qumran region.
- Troglodytes are cave dwellers.

Famous troglodytes include Makka Pakka from *In the Night Garden* and Mother Shipton.

The General Practitioners were onto the caves theme after 'Roquefort cheese', and picked up 2 points once they saw 'Dead Sea Scrolls'.

CONNECTIONS

5 points

King Oliver

3 points

Winston Churchill, Duke of London

2 points

Polly Toynbee CBE

1 point

Sir Danny Boyle

77

ANSWERS

King Oliver	Winston Churchill, Duke of London	Polly Toynbee CBE	Sir Danny Boyle

Declined honours

- Oliver Cromwell was offered the crown in February 1657. After much agonising and in the face of strong opposition from republicans and army leaders, Cromwell finally decided to reject the offer, saying, 'I will not build Jericho again.'
- Churchill was offered the title 'Duke of London' on his resignation as Prime Minister in 1955, even selecting the title himself. He was persuaded to decline it by his son Randolph. He is the last non-royal to be offered a dukedom.
- Polly Toynbee declined the CBE for services to journalism in 2000.
- Director Danny Boyle declined a knighthood for his work on the 2012 Olympic Opening Ceremony.

Among others to decline honours are Doris Lessing (damehood), Paul Weller (CBE) and Benjamin Zephaniah (OBE).

Success for the Scribblers who scored 2 points on this after very quickly asking for Clues 2 and 3 in the *Sport Relief* special against the Terriers.

5 points

Shaking a
pair of gloves

3 points

Snapping a
carrot in half

2 points

Crumpling
cellophane

1 point

Walking in
cat litter

| Shaking a pair of gloves | Snapping a carrot in half | Crumpling cellophane | Walking in cat litter |

Foley sound effects

These are traditional actions used by Foley artists to simulate sound effects frequently used in film, radio and television.

- Shaking a pair of gloves simulates the sound of a bird's wings flapping.
- Snapping a carrot in half simulates the sound of a bone breaking.
- Crumpling cellophane simulates the sound of a crackling fire.
- Walking in cat litter simulates the sound of someone walking on a gravel road.

This question taps into one of the real pleasures of *Only Connect*: no subject is off limits and the questions can shine a light onto little nuggets of 'analogue' knowledge that might otherwise get lost in our digital world.

The Numerists initially thought that these might be things done for good luck, but settled on the correct answer after seeing all four clues to score a solid 1 point.

5 points

March

3 points

The Penelopiad

2 points

Wide Sargasso Sea

1 point

Wicked

ANSWERS

| March | The Penelopiad | Wide Sargasso Sea | Wicked |

Retellings from a different character's point of view

- *March* by Geraldine Brooks (from *Little Women* by Louisa M. Alcott)
- *The Penelopiad* by Margaret Atwood (from *The Odyssey* by Homer)
- *Wide Sargasso Sea* by Jean Rhys (from *Jane Eyre* by Charlotte Brontë)
- *Wicked* by Gregory Maguire (from *The Wonderful Wizard of Oz* by L. Frank Baum)

The musical *Wicked* is based on Maguire's 1995 novel, *Wicked: The Life and Times of the Wicked Witch of the West*.

The Archers Admirers guessed 'books written about another book' and, when given another go, 'prequels', taking them further away from the correct answer, opening up the chance for the Exeter Alumni to get it right for a bonus point.

5 points

Ex-royal winner getting A1 returns (8)

3 points

Posh convict, or Ian, confined (8)

2 points

Plum sponge? (8)

1 point

Presenter of OC trivia, confusingly! (8)

| Ex-royal winner getting A1 returns (8) | Posh convict, or Ian, confined (8) | Plum sponge? (8) | Presenter of OC trivia, confusingly! (8) |

Cryptic crossword clues for VICTORIA

- Ex-royal (definition, Queen Victoria) = VICTOR (winner) + IA (A1 reversed)
- Posh (definition, Victoria Beckham) = confined in con<u>vict or Ia</u>n
- Victoria plum and Victoria sponge (double definition)
- Presenter (definition) = 'OC trivia' anagrammed (= Victoria)

For the final, it's always nice to offer special questions that don't look anything like what the contestants have seen before. Question editor at the time David Bodycombe called upon the skills of fellow *Only Connect* question writer Philip Marlow (a crossword compiler) and together they made this work so neatly. The anagram in clue 4 is particularly pleasing – maybe she was always destined to host *OC*?

The Bakers realised on Clue 2 they were cryptic crossword clues, but needed 'Plum sponge' to set them up for 2 points.

5 points

3 points

2 points

1 point

85

Nicknames for the stomach

- Bread basket
- Muffin top
- Six-pack
- Spare tyre

The Free Speakers (Ian Hislop, Simon Singh and John Sessions) picked up 2 points here in a heavyweight *Children in Need* special against the Great Believers (Nick Hornby, Dame Joan Bakewell and John Lloyd).

5 points

Agamemnon

3 points

Jim Morrison

2 points

Marion Crane

1 point

Jean-Paul Marat

| Agamemnon | Jim Morrison | Marion Crane | Jean-Paul Marat |

Died in the bath

- Agamemnon was murdered by Aegisthus (or by Clytemnestra, depending on who you believe).
- Officially, Jim Morrison of the Doors died of heart failure in the bath of his Paris flat. However, conspiracy theories abound.
- Janet Leigh's character Marion Crane is stabbed while taking a shower in a bathtub in the film *Psycho*.
- Jean-Paul Marat, a radical journalist during the French Revolution, was stabbed in the bath by Charlotte Corday, who sympathised with the moderate Girondin faction that he had denounced.

Elvis Presley, of course, died in what Americans call the bathroom, but not the bath itself.

After Clue 2 the Epicureans (who went on to win series 4) thought it was about how they died but even after Clue 3 they were doubting their knowledge, before picking up the point once they saw 'Marat'.

5 points

Kings of the Ptolemaic dynasty

3 points

Edward Heath's yachts

2 points

George Foreman's sons

1 point

Philosophy Dept, University of Woolamaloo

Kings of the Ptolemaic dynasty	Edward Heath's yachts	George Foreman's sons	Philosophy Dept, University of Woolamaloo

All have the same name

- All the Ptolemaic kings were called Ptolemy (the Queens were all called Cleopatra).
- All Heath's yachts were called *Morning Cloud*.
- All five of boxer George Edward Foreman's sons are named George Edward Foreman.
- In the Python 'Bruces sketch' everyone except the new faculty member is called Bruce.

George Foreman said, 'If you're going to get hit as many times as I've been hit by Muhammad Ali, Joe Frazier – you're not going to remember many names.'

1 point for the Bibliophiles who knew the answer after three clues, but took the last one to be sure.

5 points

dye becomes
fur

3 points

rust becomes
tidy

2 points

waxier becomes
escort

1 point

sweet becomes
derry

dye becomes fur	rust becomes tidy	waxier becomes escort	sweet becomes derry

Re-typed one key to the right

- Re-typed one key to the right

The question team spends hours mulling over which way to ask a question. For example, this one could have been fur becomes dye, tidy becomes rust, escort becomes waxier, derry becomes sweet, with the answer as 'one key to the left'. There are little clues lurking in *Only Connect* questions. For example, when the last clue of this question is revealed, the contestants should be asking themselves why 'derry' doesn't have a capital letter at the start, thus giving them a way to identify it as a word puzzle.

In the final of series 5, the Antiquarians quickly worked out this was a word puzzle, and scored 3 points – though they ended up on the losing side to the Analysts.

5 points

3 points

2 points

1 point

Colloquial units of measurement

- Nelson's Column is 52m (169ft) high in total, of which the statue is 6m (18ft).
- An Olympic swimming pool is 50m (164ft) long and holds about 2.5 million litres.
- Wales has an area of 20,779 km^2 (8,023 square miles).
- Double-decker bus; the original Routemaster was 8.4m (27.6ft) long.

The Cartophiles scored 2 points on this tricky question in the semi-final of series 7.

5 points

Self-declared king of Iceland

3 points

Prolific Welsh hymn writer

2 points

Co-writer of 'Me and Bobby McGee'

1 point

Original host of *Mastermind*

Self-declared king of Iceland	Prolific Welsh hymn writer	Co-writer of 'Me and Bobby McGee'	Original host of *Mastermind*

First name starts their surname

- Jørgen Jørgensen (seized power for two months)
- William Williams (wrote over 800 hymns)
- Kris Kristofferson (song co-written with Fred Foster and originally recorded by Roger Miller)
- Magnus Magnusson

This is slightly different from the first name being repeated in the surname – as in Neville Neville, or the character from *Barbarella*, Dr Durand Durand.

Another question from the semi-final of series 7, and again 2 points for the Cartophiles – on the way to a glorious defeat.

5 points

Oct 31

3 points

Dec 25

2 points

Hex 19

1 point

Bin 11001

Oct 31	Dec 25	Hex 19	Bin 11001

25 in different number systems

- 25 is 31 in base-8 or octal.
- 25 is 25 in base-10 or decimal.
- 25 is 19 in base-16 or hexadecimal.
- 25 is 11001 in base-2 or binary.

A fiendish question from the vaults – who could possibly not think it's about dates from the first two clues? The Heath Family were understandably led up the garden path, but worked it out by the end for 1 point.

5 points

Ford Prefect

3 points

David Brent

2 points

Sherlock Holmes

1 point

Gandalf

Ford Prefect	David Brent	Sherlock Holmes	Gandalf

Their companions are played by Martin Freeman.

- Freeman plays Arthur Dent, companion to Ford Prefect in the film of *The Hitchhiker's Guide to the Galaxy*.
- He is Tim Canterbury to Ricky Gervais's David Brent in *The Office*.
- He plays John Watson in *Sherlock*.
- In *The Hobbit* films, he plays Bilbo Baggins, hired by Gandalf.

Questions where teams need to find a connection one notch removed from the clues quite often catch teams out – but the QI Elves managed to pick up 1 point.

5 points

Formal royal
ceremonies

3 points

Those including a
religious service

2 points

Live parliamentary
proceedings
(<30 mins)

1 point

Children's
(<30 mins)

ANSWERS

| Formal royal ceremonies | Those including a religious service | Live parliamentary proceedings (<30 mins) | Children's (<30 mins) |

Advertising restrictions

- Types of TV programmes in which Ofcom does not allow adverts

Children's programmes longer than 30 minutes are allowed an advertising break. Schools' programmes are not allowed advertising breaks within the programme, but adverts are allowed between programmes.

A tricky question, but the clues gradually point towards TV. The Linguists were stumped and the Gallifreyans took the bonus point.

5 points

3 points

2 points

1 point

SI units

- HENRY VIII: the henry is the SI unit of electrical inductance.
- Boxing SECOND: the second is the SI unit of time.
- European (or common) MOLE: the mole is the SI unit of amount of substance.
- Isaac NEWTON: the newton is the SI unit of force.

We've slightly rejigged this question, but on the show the Bakers got it after seeing three clues to score 2 points.

5 points

Email newsletter for San Francisco

3 points

'Wardrobe malfunction' video not found

2 points

Selling a broken laser pointer

1 point

Harvard version of 'Hot or Not'

| Email newsletter for San Francisco | 'Wardrobe malfunction' video not found | Selling a broken laser pointer | Harvard version of 'Hot or Not' |

Inspired popular websites

- Craigslist, founded by Craig Newmark in 1995, began as a local email newsletter.
- Jawed Karim co-founded YouTube after he was unable to find a video online of the infamous Janet Jackson 'wardrobe malfunction' from the 2004 Super Bowl.
- A broken laser printer was sold online for $14.83 through Pierre Omidyar's personal website, inspiring him to launch the full eBay website.
- Mark Zuckerberg of Facebook created a short-lived site called Facemash, a version of 'Hot or Not' that allowed users to rate how attractive Harvard students were. It was so popular that it crashed Harvard's computer system and Zuckerberg had to take it down after only two weeks. He was disciplined by the university authorities.

No points for either team. The Numerists guessed '404', hoping that it might be to do with 'Page not found' on the internet. The Draughtsmen guessed 'first commercial activities of internet millionaires', which was close but not correct.

5 points

Judit Polgár

3 points

Danica Patrick

2 points

Charlotte Brew

1 point

Michelle Wie

| Judit Polgár | Danica Patrick | Charlotte Brew | Michelle Wie |

Competed in male competitions on equal terms

- At 15 years 4 months, Judit Polgár became the youngest 'men's' International Grandmaster.
- Danica Patrick was the first woman to win an IndyCar championship event.
- Charlotte Brew was the first woman to ride in a Grand National (1977, aged 21).
- Early in her career, Michelle Wie played several events on the men's PGA Tour.

Although her career began with a blaze of publicity when she was a teenager, Michelle Wie didn't win a Major Championship until 2014, when she was 24.

The Francophiles (who went on to win series 7) didn't know about Judit Polgár, but were homing in quickly with Danica Patrick. One more clue gave them the confidence to go for it and pick up 2 points.

5 points

On St Geoffrey's Day

3 points

On the Greek Calends

2 points

In the reign of Queen Dick

1 point

When Dover and Calais meet

ANSWERS

On St Geoffrey's Day	On the Greek Calends	In the reign of Queen Dick	When Dover and Calais meet

Poetic or satirical synonyms for 'never'

- There is no saint called Geoffrey.
- Calends was the first day of the month in the Roman calendar, not the Greek.
- There has been no queen called Richard.
- Dover and Calais are separated, and not just because the Channel Tunnel goes from near Folkestone.

In Shakespeare's *Macbeth*, the title character takes the phrase 'Macbeth shall never vanquished be, until Great Birnam wood to high Dunsinane hill / Shall come against him' to mean it will never happen.

1 point here for the Corpuscles as they gradually homed in the correct answer as the clues unfolded.

5 points

Jezebel

3 points

Frédéric Chopin's piano

2 points

Jan Masaryk

1 point

The Burghers of Prague

| Jezebel | Frédéric Chopin's piano | Jan Masaryk | The Burghers of Prague |

Defenestrated

They are all thought to have met their end by going through a window.

- Jezebel was thrown to her death by her own servants at the urging of Jehu, at Jezreel (2 Kings 9:33).
- Chopin's piano was thrown out of a second-floor apartment by Russian troops during the Polish uprising (January 1863).
- Czech foreign minister Jan Masaryk was thrown by persons unknown onto the courtyard of the Foreign Ministry in 1948. (Initially his death was thought to have been suicide though modern evidence points towards murder.)
- The Burghers of Prague city council were defenestrated by a mob who invaded the town hall on 30 July 1419. A second, similar event in Prague in 1618 helped to trigger the Thirty Years War.

No points for either the Trade Unionists or the Analysts, both of whom thought it was something to do with statues.

5 points

Swedish: omelette

3 points

Spanish: potato

2 points

French: marmoset

1 point

English: cheese

| Swedish: omelette | Spanish: potato | French: marmoset | English: cheese |

How photographers make their subjects smile

- *Omelett*
- *Patata*
- *Ouistiti*
- *Cheese*

Very tricky, and no shame in not having a clue about this until 'cheese'. Still, now we know the French word for marmoset.

1 point for the Alesmen, who were not in the zone at all until they had 'cheese'.

SEQUENCES

SEQUENCES

'And on to Round 2, the "Sequences" round!'

I chirrup this line in most episodes – not every episode, but often enough that it almost qualifies as a catchphrase. As catchphrases go, admittedly, it's no 'What do points make? Prizes!'

But points don't make prizes on our show anyway. Our teams win nothing but a small trophy to be shared between three. No money, no speedboats, no holidays, no appearances on the bill of the *Royal Variety Performance*. I'm not even sure they get expenses. Knowing our production manager as I do, I shouldn't be surprised if she's tricked them into smuggling themselves to Cardiff on the underside of a train.

In Round 2, the clues appear in a hidden sequence, so teams may see a maximum of three clues before working out the connection and telling us what comes fourth. If you want to know what kind of answers you should be looking for, I refer you to the comedian Mark Steel, who once tweeted: 'I love Only Connect; "the next number is 5.5, they are of course square roots of the ages of the last 4 men's Olympic taekwondo champions".'

Sadly, that is the third and final quote from Mark Steel in this book. As far as I know, he's only ever tweeted about us three times. In other words, it *isn't a sequence*. We need four. At least four.

We can, of course, create a little run of clues from sequences we find with a choice of more than four. Fans may remember the year that our former question editor Mr Connor became briefly interested in snooker, due to a BBC Three drama called *The Rack Pack* that he was writing in his spare time, and almost every sequence turned out to be four of the snooker balls in order of potting. It was a sad vision of genius under stress, like when Bobby Fischer saw every pavement as a chessboard. The caterers tried to cheer Mr Connor up by making his favourite 'traffic-light jelly' for lunch, but you can imagine how badly that turned out.

Anyway, a run or chain of potential clues with fewer than four components is useless to us. The old adage that 'bad things come in threes' takes on a new meaning for those who work on *Only Connect*.

Our question writers constantly scour the world for new sequences (I mean this figuratively: they scour via their brains and books and the internet; they do not leave their caves, I beg your pardon, their houses.)

As they scour, sequences of three make them throw up their claws, excuse me, their *hands*, in horror. But the champagne corks pop when David and Victoria Beckham have a fourth child, or Daniel Craig signs up for a fourth Bond film, or Andy Murray makes his fourth Wimbledon final. (*Come on, Andy!*)

SEQUENCES

Once again, the following questions will start
at the gentler end of the spectrum and become
progressively more difficult – and if you want to score
the round like the TV show, then you should reveal
the clues gradually. Five points if you get the answer
after one clue, three points after two clues, two
points after three clues (or one point if the opposing
team guesses for a bonus) ... and of course you can't
see four clues because *clue four is also the answer*.

Good luck!

VCM

5 points

1485

3 points

Elizabethan

2 points

Regency

?

| 1485 | Elizabethan | Regency | World War I |

Periods of the *Blackadder* series

ACCEPT: 1917 (exact setting for *Blackadder Goes Forth*)

ACCEPT: English Civil War (setting for the 1988 Comic Relief special, *Blackadder: The Cavalier Years*) as it was broadcast before *Blackadder Goes Forth*

DON'T ACCEPT: Victorian, the setting for *Blackadder's Christmas Carol*, as that was shown after *The Cavalier Years*

- 1485: *The Black Adder* (1983)
- Elizabethan: *Blackadder II* (1986)
- Regency: *Blackadder the Third* (1987)
- World War I: *Blackadder Goes Forth* (1989)

The Chessmen scored 1 point on a bonus after the Mathematicians guessed 'Battle of Bosworth'.

5 points

November

3 points

Alpha

2 points

Tango

?

November	Alpha	Tango	Oscar

'NATO' in the NATO phonetic alphabet

- November: N
- Alpha (or Alfa): A
- Tango: T
- Oscar: O

One of those satisfying questions where the answer is right there in the question – and indeed the Choir Boys quickly realised it was to do with the phonetic alphabet but they needed all three available clues before realising what was going on.

5 points

The arrival of Captain James Cook

3 points

Centaur throwing a spear of light

2 points

2,008 Fou drummers

?

| The arrival of Captain James Cook | Centaur throwing a spear of light | 2,008 Fou drummers | Queen jumps from a helicopter |

Features of Olympic opening ceremonies

ACCEPT: any feature of the 2012 London Olympics opening ceremony, e.g. Kenneth Branagh as Brunel or the Industrial Revolution

- Sydney 2000 featured the arrival of Captain James Cook.
- A centaur threw a spear of light at Athens 2004.
- Beijing 2008 had 2,008 Fou drummers.
- 'The Queen' parachuted from a helicopter at London 2012.

The Beijing opening ceremony began at 8pm on the 8th day of the 8th month, 2008. The number 8 is associated with prosperity and confidence in Chinese culture.

The Welsh Learners answered with 'Industrial Revolution' for 2 points.

5 points

4th: Portugal

3 points

3rd: Angola

2 points

2nd: Mozambique

?

| 4th: Portugal | 3rd: Angola | 2nd: Mozambique | 1st: Brazil |

Lusophone countries

These are the countries in which Portuguese is an official language, ordered by the total population of each country.

- Portugal: about 11 million people
- Angola: about 25 million people
- Mozambique: about 28 million people
- Brazil: over 200 million people

A good guess from the Gallifreyans after seeing 2nd: Mozambique secured them 2 points.

When this question was asked in series 10, official estimates had the population of Mozambique at 24 million and that of Angola at 19 million. It is quite possible that the clues of this question will need to change order in a few years!

5 points

3 points

2 points

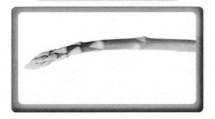

?

'Jerusalem'

ACCEPT: Scene from *Chariots of Fire*

These are the items that I demand are brought to me in the William Blake work 'And did those feet in ancient time', best known as 'Jerusalem' in its setting to the music written by Hubert Parry.

Bring me my BOW of burning gold;
Bring me my ARROWS of desire:
Bring me my SPEAR: O clouds unfold!
Bring me my CHARIOT of fire!

The Gamesmasters took a punt on 'Nuclear bombs' – but it was the Coders who scored 1 point when it came over for a bonus.

5 points

7000 → 13

3 points

13 → 8

2 points

8 → 5

?

129

| 7000 → 13 | 13 → 8 | 8 → 5 | 5 → 4 |

Quantity of letters in spelt-out numbers

- Seven thousand has 13 letters.
- Thirteen has 8 letters.
- Eight has 5 letters.
- Five has 4 letters.

Bonus question: How many letters are there in the answer to this question?

Answer: Four

The Educators scored 1 bonus point on this after the Wordsmiths were flummoxed. Victoria reckons this question is 'harder than aged pecorino cheese'.

5 points

3 points

2 points

?

Phrases starting with S, T, U and V

ACCEPT: anything preceded by V, e.g. V-sign

- S-bend
- T junction
- U-boat
- V-neck

U-boat is the anglicised version of German *U-boot*, short for *Unterseeboot* – I think you can guess what that means.

2 points for the Bowlers. They initially thought the first picture was 'Bendy road ahead', but once T-junction came up they realised the first clue was S-bend, but needed a third clue to make sure.

5 points

Galactic Centre

3 points

Sun

2 points

Earth

?

Galactic Centre	Sun	Earth	Moon

Each orbits around the previous

ACCEPT: International Space Station or any artificial satellite of Earth

- The Sun orbits around the Galactic Centre; the Earth orbits around the Sun; and the Moon orbits around the Earth.

If a team is bold enough to guess after just two clues, then an acceptable answer could be anything that orbits around any of the planets, as the sequence would then be e.g. Galactic Centre, Sun, Mars, Phobos.

No points for either team on this question in a series 8 match between the Press Gang and the Science Editors.

5 points

Possess a shotgun

3 points

Buy a National Lottery ticket

2 points

Drive a car on a public highway

?

| Possess a shotgun | Buy a National Lottery ticket | Drive a car on a public highway | Purchase alcohol |

Minimum ages of 15, 16, 17, 18

ACCEPT (e.g.): Vote, own a credit card, serve on a jury, get married without consent of parents or guardians, buy or smoke cigarettes

- Under the age of 15, a child may be in possession of a shotgun under adult supervision. From 15 they may possess a shotgun but may not hire or purchase one (i.e. they may be gifted one). There is no minimum age to possess a firearms certificate.
- You must be 16 to play the National Lottery. Under 16s may not buy a ticket or win a prize.
- A 17-year-old can drive a vehicle with no more than 8 seats and weighing less than 3,500kg.
- 18 is the minimum age for purchasing alcohol in the UK.

2 points for the Scribblers in this *Sport Relief* celebrity special. The Scribblers were Charlie Brooker, Alice Arnold and Ed Smith, and they were up against the Terriers of Clare Balding, Val McDermid and Joshua Levine.

5 points

St Petersburg

3 points

Petrograd

2 points

Leningrad

?

| St Petersburg | Petrograd | Leningrad | St Petersburg |

Successive names for St Petersburg

- St Petersburg, 1703–1914
- Petrograd, 1914–24
- Leningrad, 1924–91
- St Petersburg again, 1991 to present day

A very comfortable 3 points for the Larks (Michael Bywater, Sir Andrew Motion, Stuart Maconie) in a *Children in Need* special against the Wheel Men (Revd Richard Coles, Adam Hart-Davis, Grub Smith).

5 points

Market

3 points

Home

2 points

Roast beef

?

| Market | Home | Roast beef | None |

'This Little Piggy'

This little piggy went to MARKET,
This little piggy stayed at HOME,
This little piggy had ROAST BEEF,
This little piggy had NONE,
And this little piggy went ...
'Wee wee wee' all the way home

This was a picture question on the show, making it quite a bit harder – and indeed Brasenose Postgrads scored 0, with no bonus point for the Choir Boys either.

5 points

Wheat

3 points

Sett

2 points

Cease

?

| Wheat | Sett | Cease | Sank |

Sound like the French numbers for 8, 7, 6, 5

- Huit
- Sept
- Six
- Cinq

Something of an *Only Connect* classic, created by the show's first question editor David Bodycombe. If you don't see it, you're kicking yourself.

This completely foxed both teams: no points to either the Cricket Supporters or IT Support.

5 points

Servant of God

3 points

Venerable

2 points

Blessed

?

Servant of God	Venerable	Blessed	Saint

Process of canonisation

- *Servus Dei*
- *Venerabilis*
- *Beatus* or *Beata*
- *Sanctus* or *Sancta*

The process was instigated by Pope John Paul II in 1983. Before this there was no set process for making someone a saint.

The Bridge Players talked themselves into the correct answer for 2 points.

5 points

3 points

2 points

?

Children of the Beckhams

ACCEPT: anyone with 'Harper' in their name, e.g. former Prime Minister of Canada Stephen Harper

- BROOKLYN Bridge: Brooklyn Joseph Beckham (born 1999)
- ROMEO Montague: Romeo James Beckham (born 2002)
- Penelope CRUZ: Cruz David Beckham (born 2007)
- HARPER Lee: Harper Seven Beckham (born 2011)

3 points for the Cinephiles, though team captain (and 2009 *Mastermind* champion) Nancy Dickmann was rather embarrassed to know the answer.

5 points

4 = (e.g.) Tomato juice

3 points

5 = (e.g.) Beer

2 points

6 = (e.g.) Cow's milk

?

4 = (e.g.) Tomato juice	5 = (e.g.) Beer	6 = (e.g.) Cow's milk	7 = (e.g.) Pure water

Approximate pH scale values of acidity of various drinks

- A pH of 7 is neutral; so pure water is neutral.

A bonus point for the Chessmen after the Charity Puzzlers couldn't come up with a guess.

5 points

Thorn

3 points

Seat

2 points

Shout

?

149

Thorn	Seat	Shout	Stew

Anagrams of compass points

- Thorn = north
- Seat = east
- Shout = south
- Stew = west

No points for either team on this question in the series 1 quarter-final between the Edinburgh Scrabblers and the Crossworders.

5 points

Norman Conquest
begins

3 points

Stella Artois
brewery founded

2 points

Great Fire of
London

?

Norman conquest begins	Stella Artois brewery founded	Great Fire of London	England win the World Cup

The events are 300 years apart

ACCEPT: any notable event that happened in 1966

- Norman Conquest: 1066
- Stella Artois founded: 1366
- Great Fire of London: 1666
- England win the World Cup: 1966

Stella Artois cans have 'Anno 1366' on them. In 1366, a public house called den Horen (the Horn) started brewing in Leuven. In 1717 the Master Brewer there, Sébastien Artois, renamed it.

2 points to the Alesmen in their defeat to eventual series runners-up, the Radio Addicts (featuring 2008 and 2012 *Mastermind* champions David Clark and Gary Grant).

5 points

Noah's Ark

3 points

Jack-and-Jill
bathroom

2 points

Monty Hall
problem

?

| Noah's Ark | Jack-and-Jill bathroom | Monty Hall problem | The Doors |

Increasing number of doors

ACCEPT: 'something with four doors', 'a house with four doors', etc.

- Noah's Ark has one door.
- A shared bathroom with two doors is called a Jack-and-Jill bathroom.
- There are three doors in the Monty Hall problem.
- The Doors were a four-piece band.

The Monty Hall problem came to prominence in a reader's letter in *Parade* magazine (1990): 'Suppose you're on a game show, and you're given the choice of three doors: Behind one door is a car; behind the others, goats. You pick a door, say No. 1, and the host, who knows what's behind the doors, opens another door, say No. 3, which has a goat. He then says to you, "Do you want to pick door No. 2?" Is it to your advantage to switch your choice?'

The correct answer is 'Yes', you should switch your choice.

5 points

3: Connecticut

3 points

2: Florida

2 points

1: Maine

?

| 3: Connecticut | 2: Florida | 1: Maine | 0: Hawaii |

Number of borders with other states of the USA

ACCEPT: 0: Alaska (as it only borders Canada and no other US states)

- Connecticut borders Massachusetts, New York and Rhode Island.
- Florida borders Alabama and Georgia.
- Maine borders New Hampshire (as well as Canada).
- Hawaii is alone in the Pacific.

Missouri and Tennessee have the most borders with eight each.

After Clue 1, The History Boys thought it might be about the number of Cs (3 Cs in Connecticut), but the penny dropped when they saw Maine, so a comfortable 2 points scored.

5 points

Fear

3 points

Surprise

2 points

Ruthless
efficiency

?

| Fear | Surprise | Ruthless efficiency | Almost fanatical devotion to the Pope |

The 'three' weapons of *Monty Python*'s Spanish Inquisition

'Our *three* weapons are fear, surprise, and ruthless efficiency … and an almost fanatical devotion to the Pope. Our four … no … Amongst our weapons … Amongst our weaponry … are such elements as fear, surprise … I'll come in again.'

The speech is delivered by Cardinal Ximenez of Spain, played by Michael Palin.

This went for a bonus point in a series 3 heat between the Philosophers and the Hitchhikers.

5 points

Pack of cards

3 points

Female monarchs of Britain

2 points

Chess game

?

ANSWERS

Pack of cards	Female monarchs of Britain	Chess game	Beehive

4, 3, 2, 1 queens

ACCEPT: Anything with one queen

- A pack of cards includes the Queens of Spades, Hearts, Diamonds and Clubs.
- The female monarchs of Britain are Anne, Victoria and Elizabeth II.
- Each player in a chess game has one queen, so two in total.
- Every hive has just one queen. The old queen tends to lead the swarm just as a new queen emerges.

The United Kingdom of Great Britain did not exist until the Acts of Union of 1706 and 1707, which is why female monarchs before Anne don't count for this question.

The Ciphers scored 2 points, although the question was asked the other way – they came up with 'Two chess games being played simultaneously' for something with four queens.

5 points

3 points

2 points

?

Girls' names in the song 'Mambo No. 5'

ACCEPT: any Tina

- MONICA Lewinsky, a White House intern in the late 1990s
- ERICA Roe, probably the most famous UK streaker ever who ran on field at a 1982 England vs Australia rugby international at Twickenham
- RITA Hayworth, the actress from the Golden Age of Hollywood
- TINA Turner, the soul singer

They share names with the first four women mentioned in the chorus of Lou Bega's 1999 hit 'Mambo No. 5':

A little bit of Monica in my life
A little bit of Erica by my side
A little bit of Rita is all I need
A little bit of Tina is what I see

No points for either team, though the Press Gang identified all three pictures but suggested 'sex acts' or 'called The Body' and asked for a fourth clue – forgetting it was a Sequence question.

5 points

Millstone

3 points

Before millstone

2 points

Doglike

?

| Millstone | Before millstone | Doglike | Cutter |

Meanings of names for human teeth

These are the meanings of the names of the four categories of permanent human teeth, from the edge of the mouth to the middle.

- Millstone: molar
- Before millstone: pre-molar
- Doglike: canine
- Cutter: incisor

A dog's canines are more often called 'fangs'.

A very tough question: no points for either the Rowers or the Listeners.

5 points

Racial suffrage

3 points

Federal
income tax

2 points

Direct election to
the Senate

?

| Racial suffrage | Federal income tax | Direct election to the Senate | Prohibition of alcohol |

15th, 16th, 17th and 18th Amendments to the US Constitution

- The 15th Amendment was adopted in 1870.
- The 16th Amendment was adopted in 1913.
- The 17th Amendment was adopted in 1913.
- The 18th Amendment was adopted in 1919 and Prohibition came into force in 1920.

The 21st Amendment repealed the 18th in 1933.

Mark Labbett of the Rugby Boys was on the right track as soon as the first clue came up – though he was so excited he was told to shut up by his team captain. They scored 3 points.

5 points

2

3 points

1.73205…

2 points

1.41421…

?

| 2 | 1.73205... | 1.41421... | 1 |

Square roots of 4, 3, 2 and 1

The sequence could continue with 0 (square root of 0) and *i* (square root of -1).

The Crossworders recognised the square root of 3, and immediately cracked the puzzle for 3 points.

5 points

Move MS Word
scrollbar left

3 points

Bleaching
allowed

2 points

Play

?

Move MS Word scrollbar left	Bleaching allowed	Play	Give Way

Rotating triangles

ACCEPT: something with a triangle pointing down

The sequence describes triangles pointing in different directions, and rotating clockwise: left, up, right, down.

- A left-pointing triangular scroll arrow is used to move the MS Word scrollbar left (and indeed on other MS Office scrollbars).
- The bleaching-allowed washing symbol has a triangle pointing up.
- The play button on a media player has a triangle pointing right.
- The Give Way road sign is a red-bordered, white triangle pointing down.

2 points for the Linguists even though they couldn't think of an example; but they had solved the puzzle with their answer of 'Triangle pointing down'.

5 points

Stephen

3 points

John

2 points

Anne

?

| Stephen | John | Anne | Victoria |

Monarchs with unique regnal names

These are the English/British monarchs since 1066 with unique regnal names – Stephen and Anne were monarchs of England; Anne and Victoria were monarchs of Great Britain.

- Stephen reigned 1135–54.
- John reigned 1199–1216.
- Anne reigned 1702–14.
- Victoria reigned 1837–1901.

2 points for the In-Laws in their series 4 game against the Alesmen.

5 points

3 points

2 points

?

End in repeated vowels

ACCEPT: anything ending in double 'o'

- Laa-Laa
- Scree
- Hawaii
- Kangaroo

This question stumped both the Europhiles and the Relatives – and they even had colour to help them differentiate the Teletubbies!

5 points

Water polo

3 points

Golf foursomes

2 points

English billiards

?

Water polo	Golf foursomes	English billiards	Quidditch

Sports using 1, 2, 3, 4 balls

ACCEPT: a sport using four balls, e.g. golf fourballs, croquet

- Water polo has one ball in play at any time.
- There are two teams of two in golf foursomes; each plays a single ball alternately.
- Billiards is played with one red ball and two cue balls.
- Quidditch, the fictional sport from the world of 'Harry Potter', is played on flying broomsticks with one red Quaffle, two black Bludgers and the Golden Snitch.

The Terriers scored 2 points with their answer of 'Croquet' – even though they weren't sure it had four balls because, they said, they weren't posh.

5 points

Buenos Aires

3 points

Montevideo

2 points

Canberra

?

| Buenos Aires | Montevideo | Canberra | Wellington |

Most southerly national capital cities

- Buenos Aires is the capital of Argentina.
- Montevideo is the capital of Uruguay.
- Canberra is the capital of Australia.
- Wellington, New Zealand, is the southernmost capital of a country (and by country we mean a sovereign state that's a member of the UN in its own right).

If you allowed overseas territories, Port Stanley in the Falkland Islands would be the furthest south.

This went for a bonus point in a series 3 match between the Polymaths and the Strategists.

5 points

Pipes of Peace
1

3 points

Ebony and Ivory
2

2 points

Mull of Kintyre
3

?

ANSWERS

Pipes of Peace 1	Ebony and Ivory 2	Mull of Kintyre 3	Hey Jude 4

Solo, duo, trio, and quartet no. 1s with Paul McCartney

ACCEPT: any Beatles single that reached number one, except 'Get Back', which was credited as the Beatles with Billy Preston (a quintet)

- 'Pipes of Peace' was no. 1 for just Paul McCartney in 1983.
- 'Ebony and Ivory' was no. 1 for Paul McCartney and Stevie Wonder in 1982.
- 'Mull of Kintyre' was no. 1 for Wings (trio Paul McCartney, Linda McCartney and Denny Laine) in 1977. Biggest selling single of 1970s.
- 'Hey Jude' was the 15th of 17 no. 1s for the Beatles, the quartet that included Paul McCartney.

The Wandering Minstrels were on the right tracks, but their guess of 'barbershop quartet song and 4' opened the door for the Chessmen to score 1 bonus point as they answered 'She Loves You' for their more precise 4 person song – crucially featuring Paul McCartney.

5 points

3 points

2 points

?

Little Women

ACCEPT: any Meg or Margaret

These people share names with the March sisters from *Little Women* in ascending age order.

As described in the opening of the novel, Margaret (Meg) is sixteen, Jo is fifteen, Elizabeth (Beth) is thirteen and Amy is the youngest.

- AMY Adams, actress from *Arrival, American Hustle* and many others
- BETH Tweddle, Olympic gymnast who won bronze on asymmetric bars in 2012
- JO Brand, comedian, actress, writer
- MEG Ryan, actress, anagram of 'Germany'

The Gallifreyans identified Amy Adams immediately and gambled on people with initials such as AA, BB, CC, DD and guessed David Dimbleby. That's a question for another day. The Chessmen got to see all three clues and worked out *Little Women* on their way to the bonus point.

5 points

Starting to
develop

(– – – – – – –)

3 points

Upward
movement

(– – – – – –)

2 points

Odour

(– – – – –)

?

Starting to develop (- - - - - - -)	Upward movement (- - - - - -)	Odour (- - - - -)	Small coin (- - - -)

nascent, ascent, scent, cent

ACCEPT: unit of US currency, 100th of a dollar, French for 100, etc.

A common type of sequence question, and often very difficult to spot, though in this instance it's made a touch easier with the inclusion of the dashes to indicate number of letters. The History Boys didn't quite find the right way into the question, so it was left to the Chessmen who scored a bonus point with 'French for 100, four dashes'.

5 points

St Albans
(1980)

3 points

Bath and Wells
(1991)

2 points

Monmouth
(2002)

?

| St Albans (1980) | Bath and Wells (1991) | Monmouth (2002) | Durham (2013) |

Translations to Canterbury

They are the Dioceses from which these consecutive Archbishops of Canterbury were 'translated' (to use the Church of England term):

- Robert Runcie was translated from St Albans in 1980.
- George Carey was translated from Bath and Wells in 1991.
- Rowan Williams was translated from Monmouth in 2002.
- Justin Welby was translated from Durham in 2013.

Rowan Williams served as both Bishop of Monmouth and Archbishop of Wales simultaneously.

No points scored by either team. Gamesmasters initially thought it might be most recent cities, but homed in on Archbishops of Canterbury, and guessed 'York (2013)'. The Orienteers (series 10 champions) guessed 'Durham (2012)' for an unlucky miss. They might well have kicked themselves for not following the pattern of all clues being 11 years apart, although this was pure chance, as the position is not a fixed-term appointment.

5 points

Income Tax

3 points

VAT

2 points

Money back

?

| Income Tax | VAT | Money back | Guarantee |

Only Fools and Horses theme tune

'No Income Tax, no VAT,
No money back, no guarantee'

The show's creator John Sullivan wrote and sang both the title theme song and 'Hooky Street', which played over the closing credits. The title song was not used for the first series, but Sullivan persuaded the BBC it should be used on the second series. For one thing, it explained the origin of the title of the show.

A very quick and confident 3 points from the Strategists.

5 points

Stop sign

3 points

50p coin

2 points

Honeycomb cell

?

| Stop sign | 50p coin | Honeycomb cell | US Department of Defense building |

Polygonal shapes with 8, 7, 6, 5 sides

ACCEPT: Pentagon or anything pentagonal

- Octagon
- Heptagon (strictly, a Reuleaux heptagon due to its curved sides)
- Hexagon
- Pentagon

3 points for the Wheelmen who quickly spotted the clues were the number of sides, although two members of the team seemed confused about offering the answer 'The Pentagon', not quite realising it was fine.

5 points

Valet

3 points

Dame

2 points

Roi

?

Valet	Dame	Roi	As

French playing cards

- *Valet* = Jack
- *Dame* = Queen
- *Roi* = King
- *As* = Ace

'As' is pronounced 'ass'.

The Bowlers identified the sequence, but guessed '*un*' (going for 'one' instead of 'ace'), so it was left to the Booksellers to take the bonus point.

5 points

1st: Water jump, 3000m steeplechase

3 points

2nd: The Chair, Grand National

2 points

3rd: Tiebreak, Wimbledon Ladies' matches

?

| 1st: Water jump, 3000m steeplechase | 2nd: The Chair, Grand National | 3rd: Tiebreak, Wimbledon Ladies' matches | 4th: Vowels, *Only Connect* |

Omitted in the 1st, 2nd, 3rd, 4th part

ACCEPT: anything where the constituent is omitted in the fourth part (if you can think of anything else!)

- The water jump is not taken on the 1st lap of a 3000m steeplechase: the runners are spared the jump to give them time 'to sort themselves out'.
- The Chair is bypassed on the 2nd circuit of the Grand National.
- There is no tie break in the 3rd set of a Wimbledon Ladies' match. It's the deciding set, so players have to win by two clear games.
- The 'Missing Vowels' round is the 4th round of *Only Connect*.

Neither team scored on this question: it's a tough one to pin down. The Orienteers showed good *Only Connect* technique with their thought process: 'where people fall over?', 'an extra day?', 'happen on a special court?' before guessing: '4th: FA Cup final'. For an attempted bonus point, The QI Elves tried '4th: The Bell on a 2000m running race', using the logic that it is something that only happens in that part – the opposite of the actual answer.

5 points

3 points

2 points

?

Periods of Pablo Picasso's works

- Boy band BLUE: Blue Period, roughly 1902–4
- A ROSE: Rose Period, roughly 1905–6
- AFRICA: African Period (or Black Period), roughly 1907–9
- A sugar CUBE: Cubist Period, starting with Analytic Cubism and followed by Synthetic Cubism, roughly 1909–17

2 points for the Celts who were thinking Picasso after the first two clues.

5 points

The Premiership

3 points

Today with Des and Mel

2 points

Soccer Saturday

?

| The Premiership | Today with Des and Mel | Soccer Saturday | The Apprentice |

Previous shows of *Countdown* presenters

- Des Lynam presented *The Premiership* for ITV.
- *Today with Des and Mel* was an ITV chat show co-presented by Des O'Connor and Melanie Sykes.
- Sky Sports's *Soccer Saturday* chat and results show was anchored by Jeff Stelling, which he continued to present alongside *Countdown*.
- Nick Hewer, Lord Sugar's advisor on the BBC show *The Apprentice*, took over *Countdown* in 2012.

The original host was Richard Whiteley, who had previously hosted the Yorkshire TV news show *Calendar*.

No luck for either team on a really tough question to get your head around. The Wordsmiths came close to a bonus after it was passed over from the Wintonians but guessed '*Countdown*', not realising it was about previous shows of *Countdown* hosts.

5 points

Croesus

3 points

Benjamin Franklin's alter ego

2 points

Lazarus at the rich man's gate

?

Croesus	Benjamin Franklin's alter ego	Lazarus at the rich man's gate	A.J. Raffles

Rich Man, Poor Man, Beggar Man, Thief

ACCEPT: any well-known thief

- Croesus was King of Lydia in the sixth century BC and was famous for his wealth.
- *Poor Richard's Almanack* was an annual reference work written by Franklin under the pseudonym Poor Richard and appeared from 1732 to 1758.
- Lazarus was the diseased beggar in Jesus' parable of the rich man and the beggar.
- Arthur J. Raffles, 'the gentleman thief', was a character created in the 1890s by E.W. Hornung (a brother-in-law to Arthur Conan Doyle).

This is the second half of the 'Tinker, Tailor, Soldier, Sailor' rhyme, which is itself well-used in a variety of ingenious ways in *Only Connect*.

This question was in the final of series 8. Neither team picked up any points, though there were some great creative guesses: the Bakers went for 'a camel', thinking it might be something to do with getting through portals; the Board Gamers (the eventual champions) went for 'someone not wearing any clothes'.

5 points

5 = IV

3 points

6 = IX

2 points

7 = V

?

| 5 = IV | 6 = IX | 7 = V | 8 = I |

Roman numerals hidden in spelt-out numbers

- fIVe
- sIX
- seVen
- eIght

One of the great *Only Connect* questions: so simple, but not necessarily easy to spot, unless of course you are the Crossworders. They scored 3 points on this in a special match against members of Emmanuel College's *University Challenge*-winning team, captained by one of Victoria's favourite quizzers, Alex Guttenplan.

5 points

Black

3 points

Redmond

2 points

Regis

?

| Black | Redmond | Regis | Akabusi |

GB Men's 1991 4x400m Relay

These are the members of the 4x400m team that famously took gold at the 1991 World Championships in Tokyo.

- 1st leg: Roger Black, who won individual silver at the 1996 Olympics
- 2nd leg: Derek Redmond, perhaps most famous for being helped to the line by his father at the 1992 Olympics
- 3rd leg: John Regis, better known as a 200m runner
- 4th leg: Kriss Akabusi, 1992 Olympic 400m hurdles bronze medallist, future presenter of *Record Breakers*, former soldier, renowned laugher

Question writers work long and hard to find questions to which the answer is Kriss Akabusi – with thousands of quiz teams up and down the country called Quiz Akabusi, he's a quiz icon.

The Orienteers scored 3 points on this question, though we've made it a bit harder by removing the runners' first names. Roger Black was expected to run the final leg, and the switch paid off in the form of a gold medal and a nice *Only Connect* sequence.

5 points

Chowsingha

3 points

Triceratops

2 points

Bull

?

ANSWERS

| Chowsingha | Triceratops | Bull | Unicorn |

Creatures with 4, 3, 2, 1 horns

ACCEPT: rhinoceros or similar (although rhinoceros's horn is not a 'true' horn – it is partly made from hair – it is often referred to as such. I suppose we can't be entirely sure what a unicorn's horn is made from).

- The chowsingha is the world's only four-horned antelope, and is native to India.

The Fantasy Writers asked for Clue 2 as, quite reasonably, they had no idea about a chowsingha. Triceratops made them think it might be number of horns, with 'unicorn' as the answer, but they took the third clue anyway – and kicked themselves before securing their safe 2 points.

5 points

14: Fra Mauro

3 points

13: nowhere

2 points

12: Ocean of Storms

?

| 14: Fra Mauro | 13: nowhere | 12: Ocean of Storms | 11: Sea of Tranquillity |

Apollo moon landing sites

- Apollo 14: Shepard and Mitchell landed at Fra Mauro in 1971.
- Apollo 13: it was due to land at Fra Mauro in 1970 (which Apollo 14 later did) but the mission was aborted.
- Apollo 12: Conrad and Bean landed at the Ocean of Storms, November 1969.
- Apollo 11: Armstrong and Aldrin landed at the Sea of Tranquillity, July 1969.

A dream *Only Connect* sequence, with a very satisfactory and pertinent, though not quite giveaway, Clue 2.

The 'double l' in Sea of Tranquillity is a consistently surprising spelling.

The General Practitioners didn't really find a way into the question and guessed '11: Heaven', opening it up for the Festival Fans to score a bonus point.

5 points

4th: Play slowly

3 points

3rd: Trellick
Tower architect

2 points

2nd: Something
bestowed

?

| 4th: Play slowly | 3rd: Trellick Tower architect | 2nd: Something bestowed | 1st: Negative response |

Main villains in James Bond films

ACCEPT: anything else meaning 'No'

DON'T ACCEPT: 'cricket commentator', as Blofeld is not a main villain in *Dr No*

- Play slowly: Largo – Emilio Largo is the villain played by Adolfo Celi in *Thunderball* (1965).
- Trellick Tower architect: Ernö Goldfinger is the architect – Auric Goldfinger is the villain played by Gert Fröbe in *Goldfinger* (1964).
- Something bestowed: Grant – 'Red' Grant is the villain played by Robert Shaw in *From Russia with Love* (1963).
- Negative response: No – Dr Julius No is the villain played by Joseph Wiseman in *Dr No* (1962).

Trellick Tower is a famous block of flats near Portobello Road, west London.

No points for either the Relatives or the Europhiles on this very tricky question from the final of series 9 – the last *Only Connect* episode before the show moved from BBC Four to BBC Two.

5 points

Bath

3 points

St Patrick

2 points

Thistle

?

Bath	St Patrick	Thistle	Garter

Orders of chivalry

- Order of the Bath
- Order of St Patrick
- Order of the Thistle
- Order of the Garter

These are the most senior decorations you can wear, with the exception of the George and Victoria Crosses. The last knight of the Order of St Patrick was Prince Henry, Duke of Gloucester, who died in 1974.

An impressive 2 points from the Strategists: not much lateral thinking required here but a good display of core general knowledge.

5 points

3 points

2 points

?

Words ending ATTO, ETTO, ITTO, OTTO

Accept: anything ending OTTO, e.g. risOTTO, grOTTO, lOTTO

- Lady Sarah ChATTO: the daughter of Princess Margaret and the Earl of Snowdon; she is the Queen's only niece. Lady Sarah Armstrong-Jones married Daniel Chatto in 1994.
- A stilETTO: a shoe with a very narrow, high heel, named after the dagger
- A dITTO mark: punctuation mark indicating that something is repeated
- A mOTTO: in heraldry, a phrase or sentence accompanying a coat of arms or crest, typically on a scroll

2 points for the Relatives who didn't recognise 'Lady Sarah Chatto' but recognised 'Stiletto' and 'Beth Ditto' (whom we have mercilessly replaced with a ditto mark, though perhaps we should have gone with Ditto the Pokémon).

214

5 points

Star = G

3 points

Are = P

2 points

High = V

?

| Star = G | Are = P | High = V | Sky = Z |

'Twinkle Twinkle Little Star' = 'Alphabet Song'

Both songs are sung to the same melody, and these are the words/letters that match at the end of each line.

- 'Twinkle, twinkle, little star' = 'ABCDEFG'
- 'How I wonder what you are' = 'HIJKLMNOP'
- 'Up above the world so high' = 'QRSTUV'
- 'Like a diamond in the sky' = 'WXY and Z' (pronounced 'zee' in US)

Another version of the 'Alphabet Song' has 'Q and R and S and T' instead of 'QRSTUV' for the third line.

This brutally hard question was a reward for the Footballers and Wordsmiths in the third-place play-off of series 6. The Wordsmiths came closest with their guess of 'Low = Z' but no points.

5 points

Australian table
= 20

3 points

Table = 15

2 points

Dessert = 10

?

| Australian table = 20 | Table = 15 | Dessert = 10 | Tea = 5 |

Spoon capacity in millilitres

- Australian tablespoon capacity is 20ml.
- Standard UK tablespoon capacity is 15ml.
- Dessert spoon capacity is 10ml.
- Teaspoon capacity is 5ml.

These are the standard de facto culinary measures – all spoons are not necessarily a standard size.

Despite being initially flummoxed, the Science Editors found their way into this and picked up 2 points.

5 points

Blair elected for a
third term

3 points

The Omen remake
released

2 points

Live Earth

?

Blair elected for a third term	*The Omen* remake released	Live Earth	Beijing Olympics began

Same day/month/year

ACCEPT: any event that occurred on 08/08/08

- 05/05/05 (5 May 2005): Tony Blair wins a third General Election.
- 06/06/06 (6 June 2006): *The Omen* remake is released in cinemas, a play on the number of the Beast: 666.
- 07/07/07 (7 July 2007): The Live Earth charity concerts take place.
- 08/08/08 (8 August 2008): The Beijing Olympics officially begin at 8pm (because the Chinese like the number 8 so much).

Clue 2, though initially obscure, is very satisfactory for the evil-eyed.

A solid 2 points here for the Crossworders on their way to a convincing victory in the series 1 final.

5 points

Hanunó'o

3 points

English

2 points

Japanese

?

ANSWERS

| Hanunó'o | English | Japanese | (e.g.) Arabic |

Direction of language scripts

ACCEPT: Hebrew, Urdu or any other language that is written from right to left

DON'T ACCEPT: Chinese (if the Chinese use horizontal writing, increasingly common nowadays, it is written from left to right as in English)

Going clockwise, this is the direction in which these languages are traditionally written:

- Hanunó'o: written in vertical columns, bottom to top running from left to right
- English: written in horizontal lines, left to right
- Japanese: traditionally, and originally, written in vertical columns, top to bottom (though these days often written horizontally)
- Arabic: written in horizontal lines, right to left

Hanunó'o is one of the indigenous scripts of the Philippines.

No points for the Europhiles or the Relatives – leaving Victoria to comment, 'Welcome to the final. Isn't it horrid?'

5 points

3 points

2 points

?

Deaths of the sharks in *Jaws*

- *Jaws: The Revenge* (fourth in the series): the shark is impaled on a ship's prow.
- *Jaws 3-D* (third in the series): the pin is pulled out of a hand grenade held out by dead body inside Jaws's mouth.
- *Jaws 2*: Jaws bites into an underwater power cable winched up by Chief Brody.
- *Jaws*: Brody shoots an oxygen cylinder that Jaws is munching on.

A very tough question – especially as pictures. On the show, as a text question, the Epicureans, who went on to win the series, picked up 2 points.

5 points

Southampton

3 points

Cherbourg

2 points

Queenstown
(now Cobh)

?

Southampton	Cherbourg	Queenstown (now Cobh)	New York

Planned route of the RMS *Titanic*

ACCEPT: It sank, or similar.

- Left Southampton on 10 April 1912
- In Cherbourg to pick up passengers on evening on 10 April
- Reached Queenstown on the morning of 11 April
- Never reached New York, sank on night of 14–15 April 1912

Between 1849 and 1922, Cobh, near Cork, was called Queenstown in honour of Queen Victoria.

The Epicureans initially thought it might be about Tour de France routes, but knew it must be *Titanic* from Queenstown – so guessed 'New York' for 2 points.

CONNECTING WALLS

CONNECTING WALLS

 Hello again. When the great satirist and magazine editor Ian Hislop took part in *Only Connect* a few years ago, I introduced him as 'someone so professional that he once appeared on *Have I Got News for You* while suffering from appendicitis – considered to be the most pain a man has ever been in while recording a TV quiz … which I am personally taking as a challenge'.

I like suggesting that the experience is going to be harrowing for the contestants and, indeed, the audience at home. When I tweet the start time of an upcoming show, I usually say something to the effect that the viewer's day is about to get much worse, or point out the good news that something much more relaxing and enjoyable is on another channel at the same time.

Appearing on that charity episode with Ian Hislop was the brilliant writer-performer Mark Gatiss, of whom I said: 'Member of the League of Gentlemen, presenter of *A History of Horror*, he's a lover of all things dark and twisted – what took him so long to show up on *Only Connect*?"

When we talk about *Only Connect* being cruel, dark, twisted, etc., most people think of Round 3: the connecting wall. Each wall features sixteen clues on a grid, which can be 'solved' into four connected groups of four. The teams have two-and-a-half minutes to get it done.

That's tricky enough already, but – to make it nastier – some of the clues can fit into more than one category. 'Rover', for example, might appear on a wall that features car types, popular dog names and five-letter words. On a really horrible wall, deep into the series, you will find groups with six or even seven clues that could potentially fit – or whole fake groups that appear to be there but aren't. It works like Sudoku: whatever the false directions, there is only one complete solution with no loose ends.

That was a good line-up, wasn't it, with Mark Gatiss and Ian Hislop? Also on that episode we had the novelist and screenwriter Nick Hornby, journalist and documentary presenter Samira Ahmed, columnist and novelist Allison Pearson and the actor Stephen Mangan.

We only ever made a handful of those charity episodes – just two a year, for a few years – and I'm incredibly proud to remember who came along. It's a classy list. We resisted making them 'celebrity' episodes: some of the special guests would be recognised in any supermarket, but others' faces would not be so widely familiar. What they had in common was that they were already viewers of *Only Connect* (thus revealing a highly discriminating perspicacity), and our core viewers would probably know them, like and admire them and – crucially – respect their *ability to do the quiz*.

CONNECTING WALLS

The list included Charlie Brooker, Andrew Motion, Professor Susan Greenfield, Julian Lloyd Webber, Bonnie Greer, David Baddiel, Hugh Dennis, Professor Steve Jones, Lynne Truss, Patrick Marber, Steve Pemberton, Val McDermid, Reeta Chakrabarti, Robert Peston, Clare Balding and Simon Jenkins.

And the comedian David Mitchell, of course. He was particularly memorable.

I do think that's a list that reflects the identity of *Only Connect* very well. Surely there aren't many shows that could feature, side by side in perfect comfort, someone who's won the Royal Society Michael Faraday Prize for improving public understanding of inherited disease and genetic manipulation, and someone off *Mock the Week*.

But they were all, like the otherwise disparate people who come along to contest our main tournament, natural members of the *OC* family: bound together by their curiosity, intelligence, gamesmanship, love of BBC Four (now Two) and enthusiasm for arcane bits of fact and trivia.

Is it possible to love the fiendish connecting wall, though? Even if you think you do at the moment, let's see how you feel in a few pages' time. On the plus side, you can turn the book upside down for some extra clues you wouldn't get on the TV show.

One point for each group found, one point for each connection explained and a bonus of two points (for a maximum of ten) if you get it all correct.

Some hope.

VCM

Big Daddy	Brick	Line	Peg
Triple H	Drury	CM Punk	Maggie
Gooper	Christian	Hanger	The Undertaker
Park	Horse	Chancery	Brush

CLUE WORDS
Group 1: Big Daddy
Group 2: Christian
Group 3: Hanger
Group 4: Peg

Cat on a Hot Tin Roof characters

| Gooper | Brick | Maggie | Big Daddy |

WWE wrestlers

| Triple H | The Undertaker | Christian | CM Punk |

London 'Lanes'

| Park | Hanger | Chancery | Drury |

Clothes ____

| Horse | Peg | Line | Brush |

The Felinophiles scored 5 points on this wall in the first episode after *Only Connect* moved to BBC Two.

English breakfast	Bigga	House	Viva Forever
Yell	Goodbye	Bellow	Papa Stour
Stop	Scream	Wannabe	Caterwaul
Holler	Strength	Unst	Mainland

CLUE WORDS
Group 1: Papa Stour
Group 2: Yell
Group 3: Holler
Group 4: Stop

235

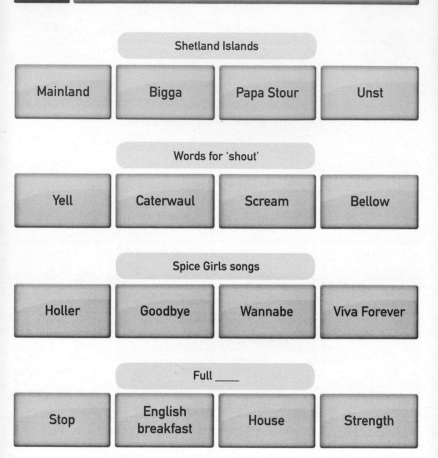

Shetland Islands

| Mainland | Bigga | Papa Stour | Unst |

Words for 'shout'

| Yell | Caterwaul | Scream | Bellow |

Spice Girls songs

| Holler | Goodbye | Wannabe | Viva Forever |

Full ____

| Stop | English breakfast | House | Strength |

The Oxonians scored 7 points on this mischievous wall, despite struggling to keep their focus as they jumped from Spice Girls to Shouting to Shetland Islands and back again.

Mop	Porterhouse	Barnet	Robinson
Grundy	Washboard	Dolly stick	T-bone
Flat iron	Strip	Malaprop	Mangle
Coiffure	Airer	Doubtfire	Do

CLUE WORDS
Group 1: Strip and Flat iron
Group 2: Dolly stick
Group 3: Grundy but not Mangle
Group 4: Mop

237

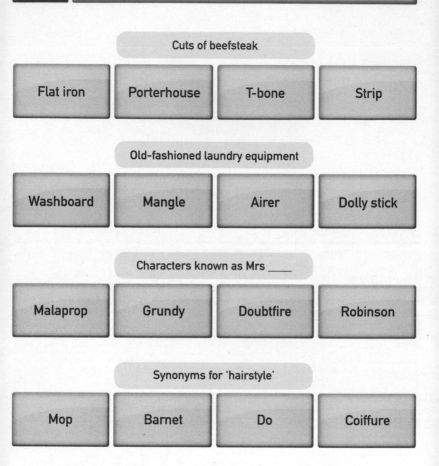

Cuts of beefsteak

| Flat iron | Porterhouse | T-bone | Strip |

Old-fashioned laundry equipment

| Washboard | Mangle | Airer | Dolly stick |

Characters known as Mrs ____

| Malaprop | Grundy | Doubtfire | Robinson |

Synonyms for 'hairstyle'

| Mop | Barnet | Do | Coiffure |

The Festival Fans solved this for an impressive 10 points.

Priest	Lawford	Knight	Pope
Kremlin	Sinatra	Martin	Bishop
Child	Deacon	Grand Slam	Hopman
Sister	Davis	Canon	Neighbour

CLUE WORDS
Group 1: Sinatra but not Davis
Group 2: Kremlin
Group 3: Not Bishop
Group 4: Sister and Child

239

The Rat Pack

| Martin | Lawford | Bishop | Sinatra |

Tennis cups

| Davis | Hopman | Grand Slam | Kremlin |

Christian clergy

| Deacon | Priest | Canon | Pope |

____hood

| Neighbour | Knight | Child | Sister |

The Erstwhile Athletes scored 7 points on this.
They managed to untangle the wall but they couldn't
identify the connection in the '____hood' group.

Wheelbarrow	Sack	Death watch	Stag
Pancake	Click	Foundation	Three-legged
Colorado	Coch	Rouge	Rosso
Bronzer	Rot	Egg-and-spoon	Goliath

CLUE WORDS

Group 1: Sack but not Pancake

Group 2: Rouge

Group 3: Rosso and Colorado

Group 4: Death watch

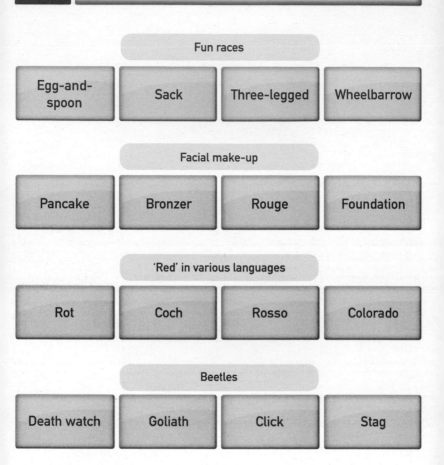

Fun races

| Egg-and-spoon | Sack | Three-legged | Wheelbarrow |

Facial make-up

| Pancake | Bronzer | Rouge | Foundation |

'Red' in various languages

| Rot | Coch | Rosso | Colorado |

Beetles

| Death watch | Goliath | Click | Stag |

A comprehensive 10 points for the Scrabblers, a celebrity team consisting of Alice Arnold, Konnie Huq and John Finnemore (who were up against the Balding Team of Clare Balding, Simon Jenkins and Clive Anderson).

Rainbow	Number 73	Button	Toronto
Kitchener	Thunder Bay	Moon	Pipkins
Hill	Ottawa	Button Moon	Hamilton
Odds	Magpie	Hunt	Hawthorn

CLUE WORDS
Group 1: Pipkins but not Rainbow
Group 2: Hamilton but not Hill
Group 3: Toronto
Group 4: Odds

243

ITV children's programmes

Magpie	Number 73	Pipkins	Button Moon

British F1 champions

Hunt	Hamilton	Button	Hawthorn

Places in Ontario, Canada

Toronto	Thunder Bay	Kitchener	Ottawa

Over the ___

Hill	Odds	Rainbow	Moon

The Gallifreyans scored 6 points on the wall. They failed to sort out 'British F1 champions' and 'Over the ___' but scored points for the connections once the wall was resolved.

Eye	Ewe	Ratio	Ration
Scrap	Sow	Boot	Hymn
Text	Compass	Jenny	Fleece
Hind	Wee	Hen	Coffee-table

CLUE WORDS
Group 1: Ewe and Eye
Group 2: Fleece but not Hind
Group 3: Sow
Group 4: Coffee-table

Homophones of pronouns

Wee	Eye	Hymn	Ewe

The Golden _____

Compass	Fleece	Ratio	Boot

Female animals

Hind	Jenny	Hen	Sow

Types of book

Scrap	Coffee-table	Ration	Text

Solved for 10 points by the Politicos.

Go West	Horn	Lust	It's a Sin
Wrath	Pride	Cod	Sex
Dry	Verde	Greed	Fear
Gluttony	Elf	Suburbia	Jealousy

CLUE WORDS

Group 1: Dry and Sex

Group 2: Wrath

Group 3: Gluttony

Group 4: Jealousy and It's a Sin

Sound like German numbers

| Dry | Fear | Sex | Elf |

Cape ____

| Wrath | Horn | Verde | Cod |

Deadly sins

| Gluttony | Greed | Lust | Pride |

Pet Shop Boys singles

| It's a Sin | Go West | Suburbia | Jealousy |

The Heath Family (captained by 2016 *Mastermind* champion Alan Heath) solved the wall, but couldn't spot the German numbers so ended up with 7 points.

Yum Yum	Asparagus	Looby Loo	PG
Hamble	Q	Madeleine	Jemima
Victoria	Raggedy Ann	Berliner	Macavity
Beignet	Bill Bailey	Churro	Felt

CLUE WORDS
Group 1: Macavity and Bill Bailey
Group 2: Hamble
Group 3: Berliner and not Madeleine
Group 4: Asparagus

Characters from *Cats*

Victoria	Bill Bailey	Jemima	Macavity

Dolls

Hamble	Looby Loo	Raggedy Ann	Madeleine

Fried dough products

Beignet	Berliner	Churro	Yum Yum

_____ tips

PG	Q	Asparagus	Felt

6 points for the Erstwhile Athletes who were close on all four groups, but only solved 'Fried dough products' and '____ tips' before confirming all four connections once the wall was resolved.

Flick	Babs	Cherry	Cluster
Micah	Temper	Ruth	Stink
Grip	Marbles	Esther	Dee Dee
Judges	Atom	Job	Bearings

CLUE WORDS
Group 1: Cluster and Cherry
Group 2: Flick and Ruth
Group 3: Esther
Group 4: Marbles

_____ bomb

| Cherry | Atom | Stink | Cluster |

Pan's People

| Dee Dee | Babs | Flick | Ruth |

Books of the Old Testament

| Judges | Esther | Job | Micah |

Things you can lose

| Marbles | Temper | Bearings | Grip |

A very impressive 10 points for the Draughtsmen, who needed just 57 seconds to sort out this wall.

Shaft	Rockford	Cuff	Cannon
Breast	Ironside	Pocket	Éclair
Kiss	Bridge	Vent	Lapel
Baulk	Neige	Plant	Glace

CLUE WORDS
Group 1: Éclair and Vent
Group 2: Pocket
Group 3: Baulk but not Cannon
Group 4: Ironside

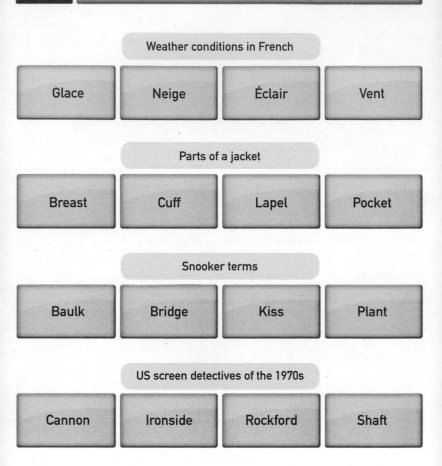

Weather conditions in French

| Glace | Neige | Éclair | Vent |

Parts of a jacket

| Breast | Cuff | Lapel | Pocket |

Snooker terms

| Baulk | Bridge | Kiss | Plant |

US screen detectives of the 1970s

| Cannon | Ironside | Rockford | Shaft |

The Lasletts solved this in just 36 seconds, picking up the full 10 points.

Styles	Orient Express	Horan	Wigeon
Merganser	Puffing Billy	The Nile	Tomlinson
Eider	Mesopotamia	Flying Scotsman	Malik
Mallard	Payne	Rocket	Teal

CLUE WORDS

Group 1: Tomlinson

Group 2: Styles and Orient Express

Group 3: Rocket

Group 4: Teal but not Mallard

ANSWERS

One Direction

| Malik | Tomlinson | Horan | Payne |

Poirot locations

| Mesopotamia | Styles | The Nile | Orient Express |

Steam locomotives

| Mallard | Flying Scotsman | Rocket | Puffing Billy |

Ducks

| Merganser | Teal | Wigeon | Eider |

7 points for the Bibliophiles who found all the connections apart from One Direction – prompting much giggling from the host.

Browning	Stansted	Tennyson	Regan
Duke of Cornwall	Hopkins	Arnold	Lear
Prestwick	Majority	John Lennon	Heathrow
Goneril	Mayor	George Best	Oswald

CLUE WORDS
Group 1: Mayor and Browning
Group 2: Lear and Tennyson
Group 3: Stansted
Group 4: Goneril

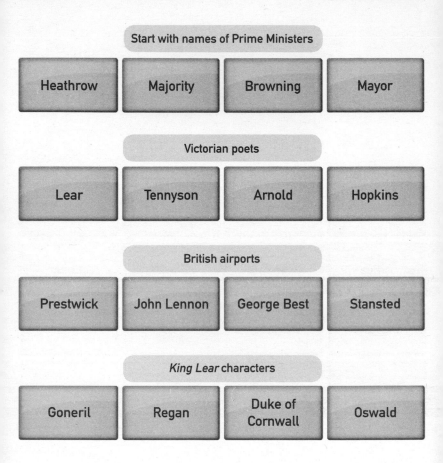

Start with names of Prime Ministers

| Heathrow | Majority | Browning | Mayor |

Victorian poets

| Lear | Tennyson | Arnold | Hopkins |

British airports

| Prestwick | John Lennon | George Best | Stansted |

King Lear characters

| Goneril | Regan | Duke of Cornwall | Oswald |

The QI Elves solved this for 10 points in the semi-final – albeit without a couple of little changes to show due deference to Theresa May (on the show they had 'Pittsburgh' rather than 'Mayor') and George Best (in place of 'Robin Hood' – as that is now properly known as Doncaster Sheffield).

Liver	Nightmare	Avid	Uke
Ames	Rhodes	Evans	Downton
Clavinet	Wurlitzer	Baldwin Combo	Northanger
Thélème	Redwall	CP-70	Parks

CLUE WORDS
Group 1: Northanger but not Downton
Group 2: Rhodes
Group 3: Wurlitzer
Group 4: Ames and Uke

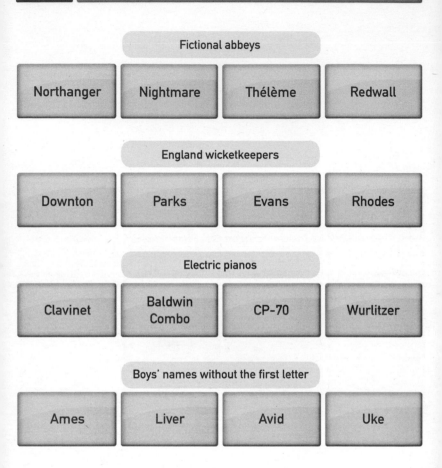

Fictional abbeys

| Northanger | Nightmare | Thélème | Redwall |

England wicketkeepers

| Downton | Parks | Evans | Rhodes |

Electric pianos

| Clavinet | Baldwin Combo | CP-70 | Wurlitzer |

Boys' names without the first letter

| Ames | Liver | Avid | Uke |

6 points for the Orienteers on this exceptionally hard wall in the semi-final of series 10. The Orienteers went on to win the series, meaning that Sean Blanchflower (their captain) became the first (and so far only) person to do the *University Challenge* and *Only Connect* double. He won *University Challenge* with Trinity College, Cambridge, in the first series of the Paxman era.

Bow Street	Mayfair	Blade	Long distance
Whitehall	Pall Mall	Mandarin	Black
Piccadilly	London	Camel	Buster Brown
Strand	Road	Daniel	Ruff

CLUE WORDS
Group 1: Mandarin and Ruff
Group 2: Camel
Group 3: Whitehall and Black
Group 4: Long distance

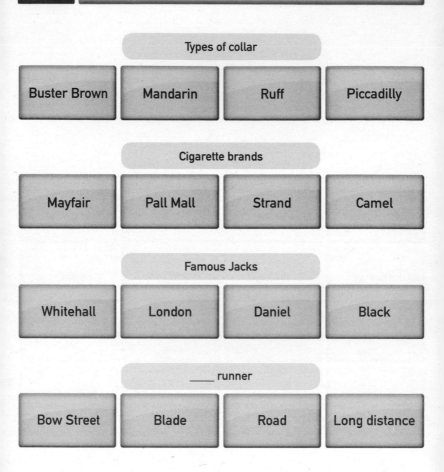

Types of collar

| Buster Brown | Mandarin | Ruff | Piccadilly |

Cigarette brands

| Mayfair | Pall Mall | Strand | Camel |

Famous Jacks

| Whitehall | London | Daniel | Black |

____ runner

| Bow Street | Blade | Road | Long distance |

The Orienteers cracked this fiendish wall for the maximum 10 points in the series 10 final after quickly identifying that there were simply too many London streets (and as it turns out, they are a false group).

Pending	Perfect	Lively	Pitstop
Frieze	Zulu	Berber	Slag
Cruz	Wilton	Spheeris	Igbo
Fulani	Amhara	Cut and loop	Axminster

CLUE WORDS
Group 1: Zulu
Group 2: Axminster
Group 3: Cruz and Spheeris
Group 4: Pitstop and Slag

263

ANSWERS

Ethnic groups in Africa

| Igbo | Amhara | Fulani | Zulu |

Types of carpet

| Cut and loop | Frieze | Berber | Axminster |

Famous Penelopes

| Cruz | Spheeris | Lively | Wilton |

***Wacky Races* drivers**

| Pitstop | Perfect | Pending | Slag |

The Wrights faced this during a special *Only Connect* Wall Night. They spotted most of the groups quite early, but couldn't find a way to make it work, and ended up with 4 points.

Love	Mize	Phis	Toms
Room	Seta	Kite	Pate
Etas	File	Psis	East
Teas	Eats	Seat	Rhos

CLUE WORDS
Group 1: East
Group 2: File and Seat
Group 3: Etas
Group 4: Mize and Love

Anagrams of each other

East	Eats	Teas	Seta

Box ____

Seat	Room	Kite	File

Plurals of Greek letters

Etas	Psis	Rhos	Phis

American Major-winning golfers

Toms	Mize	Love	Pate

Part of a pair of evil walls packed with four-letter words used in the final of series 9. On this one, the Relatives scored 6 points after spending some time successfully sorting out the anagrams.

Hole	Mole	Pole	Pots
Spot	Tops	Prop	Pock
Race	Test	Rate	Wart
Stop	Opts	Post	Mast

CLUE WORDS
Group 1: Opts
Group 2: Prop and Post
Group 3: Rate and Race
Group 4: Spot

Anagrams of each other

| Opts | Pots | Stop | Tops |

Supporting structures

| Post | Pole | Prop | Mast |

_____ card

| Hole | Rate | Race | Test |

Skin blemishes

| Spot | Mole | Wart | Pock |

Part of a pair of evil walls packed with four-letter words used in the final of series 9. On this one, the Europhiles (who won the series) salvaged 3 points having failed to sort any connections during the allocated time.

The	Only Connect	Quiz	Book
Grill	Silk	Talk	Probe
Hadrian's	Duran	Earth	Antonine
Everything	Interrogate	Berlin	Inch

CLUE WORDS

Group 1: The
Group 2: Only Connect
Group 3: Quiz
Group 4: Book

Repeated band names

| The | Duran | Talk | Everything |

Famous walls

| Only Connect | Hadrian's | Berlin | Antonine |

To question

| Quiz | Grill | Interrogate | Probe |

____worm

| Book | Earth | Silk | Inch |

There are occasionally hidden messages in Walls on the show – though usually so well hidden that nobody notices.

Rope	Killer	Vertigo	Beluga
Sperm	Rear Window	Candlestick	Suspension
Dagger	Bascule	Minke	Revolver
Humpback	Spanner	Swing	Psycho

CLUE WORDS

Group 1: Candlestick
Group 2: Rope
Group 3: Humpback
Group 4: Killer

ANSWERS

Cluedo weapons

| Spanner | Dagger | Candlestick | Revolver |

Alfred Hitchcock films

| Rope | Rear Window | Vertigo | Psycho |

Bridges

| Bascule | Humpback | Swing | Suspension |

Whales

| Killer | Sperm | Minke | Beluga |

Sherry	Boxer	Port	Bermuda
Waves	Saint Helena	Cycling	Vermouth
Lanzarote	Craft	Marsala	Brush
Beach	Madeira	Rugby	Ascension

CLUE WORDS
Group 1: Madeira
Group 2: Port
Group 3: Bermuda
Group 4: Boxer

273

Fortified wines

Sherry   Madeira   Marsala   Vermouth

Air _____

Port   Waves   Craft   Brush

Islands in the Atlantic

Bermuda   Lanzarote   Saint Helena   Ascension

Types of shorts

Boxer   Cycling   Beach   Rugby

Rush	Hindhead	Marsh	Blackwall
Dartford	Heighway	Apollo 13	Gerrard
Fowler	Reed	Channel	Willow
Cocoon	Box	Dalglish	A Beautiful Mind

CLUE WORDS
Group 1: Gerrard
Group 2: Rush
Group 3: Dartford
Group 4: Channel

Former Liverpool FC players

Fowler	Gerrard	Dalglish	Heighway

Films directed by Ron Howard

Rush	Apollo 13	Cocoon	A Beautiful Mind

Types of warbler

Willow	Marsh	Reed	Dartford

Tunnels

Hindhead	Blackwall	Box	Channel

Monster	Cox	There	Pickup
Eno	Whammy bar	Dump	Blessed
Garbage	Rouf	Clough	Flatbed
Bridge	Lara	Fretboard	Tow

CLUE WORDS
Group 1: Monster
Group 2: Pickup
Group 3: Eno
Group 4: Clough

ANSWERS

Trucks

Flatbed | Dump | Garbage | Monster

Parts of an electric guitar

Fretboard | Pickup | Bridge | Whammy bar

Anagrams of numbers

Eno | Tow | There | Rouf

Brians

Cox | Clough | Lara | Blessed

Neon	Drood	Argon	Copperfield
Gallifrey	Daniels	Vulcan	Radon
Rudge	Krypton	Dynamo	Chuzzlewit
Zenon	Twist	Helium	Tatooine

CLUE WORDS
Group 1: Neon
Group 2: Krypton
Group 3: Copperfield
Group 4: Rudge

Noble gases

| Neon | Argon | Helium | Radon |

Fictional planets

| Krypton | Gallifrey | Vulcan | Tatooine |

Magicians

| Zenon | Daniels | Copperfield | Dynamo |

Eponymous Dickens characters

| Rudge | Drood | Twist | Chuzzlewit |

Planet Earth	London	Africa	The Reflex
Montreal	Save a Prayer	Cat's	Sydney
Private	Zoo Quest	Atlanta	Frozen Planet
Munich	Ordinary World	Naked	Rio

CLUE WORDS
Group 1: Montreal
Group 2: Rio
Group 3: Planet Earth
Group 4: London

Non-capital city Summer Olympic venues

Montreal	Munich	Atlanta	Sydney

Duran Duran songs

Ordinary World	Save a Prayer	Rio	The Reflex

David Attenborough documentaries

Planet Earth	Frozen Planet	Zoo Quest	Africa

____ eye

London	Private	Naked	Cat's

Caesar	Cinch	Hurricane	Pushover
Mistral	Greek	Child's play	Gale
Piece of cake	Sirocco	Peeta	Potato
Waldorf	Katniss	Cobb	Breeze

CLUE WORDS

Group 1: Caesar
Group 2: Breeze
Group 3: Cinch
Group 4: Greek

283

The Hunger Games characters

Caesar	Katniss	Peeta	Gale

Winds

Mistral	Sirocco	Hurricane	Breeze

Easy

Piece of cake	Cinch	Child's play	Pushover

Salads

Waldorf	Greek	Cobb	Potato

Rose	Sclera	Wood	Tulip
Flute	Daisy	Cornea	Onslow
Iris	Highball	Hyacinth	Donald
Emmet	Casey	Pupil	Rummer

CLUE WORDS
Group 1: Casey
Group 2: Onslow
Group 3: Cornea
Group 4: Highball

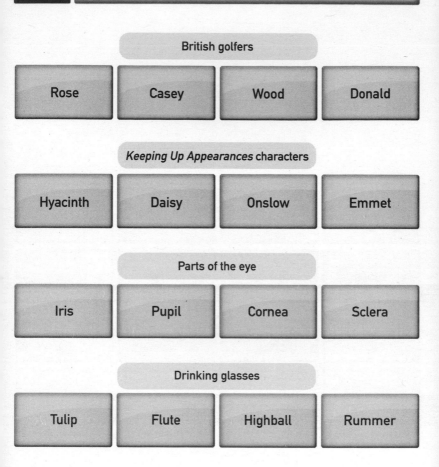

British golfers

| Rose | Casey | Wood | Donald |

Keeping Up Appearances characters

| Hyacinth | Daisy | Onslow | Emmet |

Parts of the eye

| Iris | Pupil | Cornea | Sclera |

Drinking glasses

| Tulip | Flute | Highball | Rummer |

This wall is made rather trickier if you spend too long on the false group of flowers: Rose, Hyacinth, Daisy, Iris, Tulip.

Pollock	Scuttle	Brill	Trimmer
Ariel	Sole	Prince Eric	Lichtenstein
Warhol	Sebastian	Brush	Turbot
Flounder	Razor	Hopper	Ursula

CLUE WORDS
Group 1: Pollock
Group 2: Flounder
Group 3: Ursula
Group 4: Scuttle

American artists

| Pollock | Warhol | Hopper | Lichtenstein |

Flatfish

| Flounder | Sole | Brill | Turbot |

Characters from *The Little Mermaid*

| Ariel | Sebastian | Ursula | Prince Eric |

Shaving equipment

| Razor | Brush | Scuttle | Trimmer |

Cork	Pickle	Albright	Galway
Piccalilli	Rice	Clare	Scrape
Fix	Mayo	Kissinger	Pesto
Kerry	Quandary	Horseradish	Dilemma

CLUE WORDS
Group 1: Mayo
Group 2: Kerry
Group 3: Pickle
Group 4: Dilemma

ANSWERS

Counties of Ireland

Cork	Mayo	Clare	Galway

US Secretaries of State

Kerry	Rice	Albright	Kissinger

Condiments

Piccalilli	Horseradish	Pickle	Pesto

Tricky situations

Fix	Dilemma	Quandary	Scrape

Dee	Challis	Nith	Calico
Picnic	Clyde	Denim	Peel
Tweed	Wogan	Moses	Don
Wastepaper	Corduroy	Everett	Linen

CLUE WORDS
Group 1: Dee
Group 2: Tweed
Group 3: Denim
Group 4: Linen

Original BBC Radio 1 DJs

| Dee | Wogan | Everett | Peel |

Rivers in Scotland

| Tweed | Clyde | Nith | Don |

Fabrics

| Challis | Corduroy | Denim | Calico |

_____ basket

| Linen | Wastepaper | Picnic | Moses |

Argyle	Aquitaine	Gomez	Brunswick
Mint	Morticia	Alexandra	Uncle Fester
Wednesday	Olive	Braganza	Villa
Cleves	Lurch	Forest	Teck

CLUE WORDS
Group 1: Wednesday
Group 2: Brunswick
Group 3: Cleves
Group 4: Lurch

293

Football team suffixes

| Argyle | Wednesday | Alexandra | Villa |

Shades of green

| Mint | Olive | Forest | Brunswick |

Royal consorts

| Aquitaine | Cleves | Braganza | Teck |

Characters from *The Addams Family*

| Lurch | Gomez | Uncle Fester | Morticia |

Code	Mull	Bolt	Egg
Skye	Rivet	Joke	Owens
Staple	Gatlin	Iona	Linchpin
Lewis	Nut	Christie	Jura

CLUE WORDS
Group 1: Nut
Group 2: Bolt
Group 3: Lewis
Group 4: Iona

Things that can be cracked

| Code | Nut | Joke | Egg |

Fasteners

| Bolt | Staple | Rivet | Linchpin |

Sprinters

| Gatlin | Christie | Lewis | Owens |

Islands of the Hebrides

| Skye | Mull | Iona | Jura |

On My Own	Cable	I Dreamed a Dream	Maple Leafs
Barleycorn	Red Wings	Of attorney	One Day More
Station	Who Am I?	Bruins	Light year
Stars	Struggle	Fathom	Rangers

CLUE WORDS
Group 1: On My Own
Group 2: Stars
Group 3: Rangers
Group 4: Cable

Songs from *Les Misérables*

| On My Own | Who Am I? | I Dreamed a Dream | One Day More |

NHL ice hockey teams

| Stars | Red Wings | Bruins | Maple Leafs |

Power ____

| Rangers | Station | Struggle | Of attorney |

Units of length

| Cable | Barleycorn | Fathom | Light year |

Jamb	Bark	Lakes	Dental
Britain	Open heart	Hinge	Dane
Plastic	Handle	Grandfather	Lintel
Keyhole	Expectations	List	Laser

CLUE WORDS
Group 1: Keyhole
Group 2: Britain
Group 3: Grandfather
Group 4: Dental

Parts of a door

Jamb	Keyhole	Hinge	Lintel

Homophones for composers

Handle	Bark	Britain	List

Great _____

Expectations	Lakes	Grandfather	Dane

Types of surgery

Plastic	Dental	Open heart	Laser

Trolley	Bull	Frozen foods	Oche
Arrows	Fish counter	Double top	Alert
Twins	Herring	Scales	Aisle
Checkout	Water carrier	Wire	Pepper

CLUE WORDS
Group 1: Checkout
Group 2: Arrows
Group 3: Bull
Group 4: Trolley

Terms in darts

| Double top | Oche | Wire | Checkout |

Red ____

| Pepper | Herring | Alert | Arrows |

Zodiac symbols

| Bull | Scales | Water carrier | Twins |

Found in a supermarket

| Trolley | Aisle | Fish counter | Frozen foods |

Homily	Entendre	Arrietty	Oration
Bloom	Eulogy	School	Hendreary
Sermon	Glazing	Lecture	Bed
Dutch	Pod	Negative	Shoal

CLUE WORDS
Group 1: Pod
Group 2: Shoal
Group 3: Lecture
Group 4: Glazing

Borrowers

| Arrietty | Pod | Homily | Hendreary |

Groups of sea creatures

| Bloom | Shoal | School | Bed |

Words for 'a speech'

| Sermon | Lecture | Eulogy | Oration |

Double ____

| Dutch | Entendre | Glazing | Negative |

Gold	Cassini	Clown	Galileo
Matelot	Utah	Tar	Sword
Jelly	Mariner	Blow	Bluejacket
Juno	Cuttle	Omaha	Voyager

CLUE WORDS
Group 1: Gold
Group 2: Jelly
Group 3: Mariner
Group 4: Juno

305

D-Day landing beaches

| Gold | Utah | Omaha | Sword |

_____ fish

| Jelly | Cuttle | Clown | Blow |

Sailors

| Mariner | Tar | Matelot | Bluejacket |

Space probes

| Cassini | Voyager | Juno | Galileo |

Park	Todd	Speke	Fisher
Fortensky	Bowie	Tiggy-Winkle	Palette
Nutkin	Livingstone	Bread	Burton
Stanley	Puddle-Duck	Hilton	Bland

CLUE WORDS
Group 1: Burton
Group 2: Fisher
Group 3: Puddle-Duck
Group 4: Stanley

Explorers of Africa

Park	Livingstone	Speke	Burton

Husbands of Elizabeth Taylor

Hilton	Todd	Fisher	Fortensky

Beatrix Potter characters

Tiggy-Winkle	Puddle-Duck	Nutkin	Bland

Knives

Stanley	Bowie	Bread	Palette

MISSING VOWELS

MISSING VOWELS

 If I were a contestant on *Only Connect*, I'd be the type who remains largely silent throughout the show – quiet and motionless on the end of the row, eyes darting nervously about, increasingly morose, contributing nothing to the early rounds – then comes alive for the Missing Vowels.

BUZZ, '*Das Kapital*!'

BUZZ, 'Chim Chim Cheree!'

BUZZ, 'Saving Private Ryan O'Neal!'

If you've seen the show, you'll know the type I mean. Some of us can do Round 4 quite easily, even if we find the rest of the quiz nearly impossible.

The truth is that deciphering the original lines and phrases from which the vowels have been removed (and consonants re-spaced) is a completely different discipline from the rest of the programme. It's not really about connecting. We can get away with including it because the clues come in connected sets of four (so you *could* solve them by thinking laterally and guessing which US state or Etruscan philosopher or husband of Zsa Zsa Gabor is likely to be included) but that's a pretty thin rationale. The round's just there to make things seem a bit different.

I know I'm not supposed to say that. On *QI*, they don't say: 'Now it's time for "General Ignorance", which is exactly like the rest of the show but has a different name in the interests of apparent variety.'

On *They Think It's All Over*, Nick Hancock never said: 'And now it's time for "Feel the Sportsman", a round which has been spuriously included in order to inject some physical comedy into the proceedings.'

I'm not criticising either of those excellent quizzes. I don't think there's anything wrong with spurious rationales for rounds. This is entertainment, not the criminal justice system. None of it matters.

But I enjoy deconstructing bits of the show out loud, mainly because our viewers are (a) very bright and (b) constantly thinking, calculating and analysing, so they will already have done a fair bit of deconstruction themselves. It's good to surprise them by joining in.

That's the point of my remarks at the beginning and end of each episode, which have become odder and more involved over the years (and sometimes funnier, though certainly not all of the time).

All I really need to say is 'Hello and welcome to *Only Connect*' at the beginning of each show and 'Thanks for watching. Goodbye' at the end. That's all I *did* say for the first couple of series, as I remember.

But as time wore on and I racked up more and more appearances in the host's chair, those opening pleasantries started to feel sillier and hollower – just as a word starts to seem strange in your mind if you say it often enough. (Try it with 'milk'. That will go peculiar quite quickly.)

And I assumed that our thoughtful, bright, analytical viewers were equally aware that I was mouthing pleasantries for the sake of form, and might feel disappointed that an otherwise quirky and challenging show could do something so first base and predictable.

So, I started making my opening remarks very quickly, or very slowly, or skipping the 'Hello' and starting in the middle of a sentence. Sometimes the remarks would be about something I'd left in my dressing room, or found on the floor, or what I'd had to drink, or a daydream I was having about Michael Portillo.

In 2016, everything I said in the opening minutes of the first 19 episodes was on a Scottish theme. I talked about Sean Connery, Celtic and Rangers, lucky heather, Rod Stewart, McWomble.

I quoted Rabbie Burns, explaining he was 'very much Scotland's answer to the poet Robert Burns'.

'Welcome to Only Connect,' I shouted, 'where – much like a night with the Krankies – everything's up for grabs!'

Very few people noticed. But the ones who did were pleased: they'd spotted a whole other set of hidden connections. I kept it up for 19-odd shows, then never mentioned Scotland again for the rest of the series.

It was all totally arbitrary, but (like most of my opening and closing remarks) I meant it to be, at some level, a comment on the arbitrary principle of opening and closing remarks.

Some people hate those bits of the show. Others love them. Many more, I'm sure, are deaf to them, simply waiting for the quiz to start. That's sort of the point, really.

Anyway, these are my closing remarks for this book because I'm bowing out before Round 4, which is about to start. Good luck: you get one point for each correctly deciphered line or phrase, and you *lose* a point for any incorrect guess.

After Round 4, you will find an 'audition paper'. But you won't find the answers to the audition paper, only a web address where you can send your best submission.

I'm not sure whether or not anybody will get back to you. They may simply steal your data and sell it on to unscrupulous third parties in Nigeria. If they think you're brilliant, perhaps they will invite you on to the series. If *you* think you're brilliant, why not get in touch with Parasol Media and invite yourself on?

Why not? I'd love to meet you. We always need new victims, I beg your pardon, contestants. And let's be honest, you're the sort of person who buys an *Only Connect* book. It's not like you've got anything else to do.

VCM

Nursery rhymes

NTWB CKLM YSH

LDK NGC L

PPG STHW SL

RNG SN DLM NS

Nursery rhymes

NTWB CKLM YSH

ONE, TWO, BUCKLE MY SHOE

LDK NGC L

OLD KING COLE

PPG STHW SL

POP GOES THE WEASEL

RNG SN DLM NS

ORANGES AND LEMONS

Hairstyles

SH RTB CKN DSDS

B H V

FR

T NCR P

Hairstyles

SH RTB CKN DSDS

SHORT BACK AND SIDES

B H V

BEEHIVE

FR

AFRO

T NCR P

ETON CROP

The song title is not mentioned in its lyrics

T HBL LD FJH NND YK

V VLV D

FLRS CNT DL SCNT

SML LSL KTNS PRT

ANSWERS

The song title is not mentioned in its lyrics

T HBL LD FJH NND YK

THE BALLAD OF JOHN AND YOKO

V VLV D

VIVA LA VIDA

FLRS CNT DL SCNT

FLUORESCENT ADOLESCENT

SML LSL KTNS PRT

SMELLS LIKE TEEN SPIRIT

These are songs by:

- The Beatles
- Coldplay
- Arctic Monkeys
- Nirvana

Things people say when breaking up

TSNT YT SM

WSH LDS THRP PL

NDS MSPC

CNWS TLL BFR NDS

Things people say when breaking up

TSNT YT SM

IT'S NOT YOU, IT'S ME

WSH LDS THRP PL

WE SHOULD SEE OTHER PEOPLE

NDS MSPC

I NEED SOME SPACE

CNWS TLL BFR NDS

CAN WE STILL BE FRIENDS?

15-letter words

NT RP RNR L

PHT HLML GST

NSCR TN BL

M PR SSN STC

15-letter words

NT RP RNR L

ENTREPRENEURIAL

PHT HLML GST

OPHTHALMOLOGIST

NSCR TN BL

UNASCERTAINABLE

M PR SSN STC

IMPRESSIONISTIC

Said by magicians

PC KCR DNYC RD

J STLK TH T

ZZ YW ZZ YLTS GTBSY

BRCD BR

ANSWERS

Said by magicians

PC KCR DNYC RD

PICK A CARD, ANY CARD

J STLK TH T

JUST LIKE THAT

ZZ YW ZZ YLTS GTBSY

IZZY WIZZY, LET'S GET BUSY

BRCD BR

ABRACADABRA

326

Chemicals used at home

CS TCS D

PS MS LTS

T RPN TN

LFW NTR GRN

Chemicals used at home

CS TCS D

CAUSTIC SODA

PS MS LTS

EPSOM SALTS

T RPN TN

TURPENTINE

LFW NTR GRN

OIL OF WINTERGREEN

Films starring married couples

YS WDS HT

KYL RG

THG TW Y

W HSF RD FVR GNW LF

Films starring married couples

YS WDS HT

EYES WIDE SHUT

KYL RG

KEY LARGO

THG TW Y

THE GETAWAY

W HSF RD FVR GNW LF

WHO'S AFRAID OF VIRGINIA WOOLF?

The married couples were:

- Nicole Kidman and Tom Cruise
- Lauren Bacall and Humphrey Bogart
- Kim Basinger and Alec Baldwin
- Elizabeth Taylor and Richard Burton

Four names for the same thing

PNT HR

C G R

MNT NLN

PM

Four names for the same thing

PNT HR

PANTHER

C G R

COUGAR

MNT NLN

MOUNTAIN LION

PM

PUMA

Things removed in the game 'Operation'

B RKNH RT

FN NYB N

BTTR FLSN THST MCH

D MS PPL

Things removed in the game 'Operation'

B RKNH RT

BROKEN HEART

FN NYB N

FUNNY BONE

BTTR FLSN THST MCH

BUTTERFLIES IN THE STOMACH

D MS PPL

ADAM'S APPLE

Sportspeople merged with music acts

FRNK BR NM RS

LRR BSNN DJ RM

RG RBL CKY DPS

RBBS VGG RDN

Sportspeople merged with music acts

FRNK BR NM RS

FRANK BRUNO MARS

LRR BSNN DJ RM

LAURA ROBSON AND JEROME

RG RBL CKY DPS

ROGER BLACK EYED PEAS

RBBS VGG RDN

ROBBIE SAVAGE GARDEN

Foods and their North American names

BRG NN DGG PLNT

CR GTTN DZC CHN

CRN DRN DCL NTR

BS CTN DCK

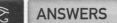

Foods and their North American names

BRG NN DGG PLNT

AUBERGINE AND EGGPLANT

CR GTTN DZC CHN

COURGETTE AND ZUCCHINI

CRN DRN DCL NTR

CORIANDER AND CILANTRO

BS CTN DCK

BISCUIT AND COOKIE

Attributed famous last words

TTB RT

SHL LHR NHV N

G TM YSW NCS TMR DY

BG GRB GNR

Attributed famous last words

TTB RT

ET TU, BRUTE?

SHL LHR NHV N

I SHALL HEAR IN HEAVEN

G TM YSW NCS TMR DY

GET MY SWAN COSTUME READY

BG GRB GNR

BUGGER BOGNOR

These are the last words attributed to:

- Julius Caesar
- Ludwig van Beethoven
- Anna Pavlova
- King George V

Two names for the same chemical element

QC KSLV RNDM RCRY

SPLT RNDZ NC

WLF RMN DTNG STN

NTRM NDS DM

Two names for the same chemical element

QC KSLV RNDM RCRY

QUICKSILVER AND MERCURY

SPLT RNDZ NC

SPELTER AND ZINC

WLF RMN DTNG STN

WOLFRAM AND TUNGSTEN

NTRM NDS DM

NATRIUM AND SODIUM

Words that contain all five vowels only once

DC TN

THR S

S Q

BST MS

ANSWERS

Words that contain all five vowels only once

DC TN

EDUCATION

THR S

AUTHORISE

S Q

SEQUOIA

BST MS

ABSTEMIOUS

Rudyard Kipling's *Just So Stories*

THC TT HTW LKDB YHM SLF

HWT HLP RDG THS SPTS

THC RBT HTPL YDW THT HS

H WTH CMLG THS HMP

Rudyard Kipling's *Just So Stories*

THC TT HTW LKDB YHM SLF

THE CAT THAT WALKED BY HIMSELF

HWT HLP RDG THS SPTS

HOW THE LEOPARD GOT HIS SPOTS

THC RBT HTPL YDW THT HS

THE CRAB THAT PLAYED WITH THE SEA

H WTH CMLG THS HMP

HOW THE CAMEL GOT HIS HUMP

(Reasons it's fun to stay at the) YMCA

YC NGTY RSLFC LN

YC ND WH TVR YFL

YC N HVG DML

YC NH NGTW THLL THB YS

(Reasons it's fun to stay at the) YMCA

YC NGTY RSLFC LN

YOU CAN GET YOURSELF CLEAN

YC ND WH TVR YFL

YOU CAN DO WHATEVER YOU FEEL

YC N HVG DML

YOU CAN HAVE A GOOD MEAL

YC NH NGTW THLL THB YS

YOU CAN HANG OUT WITH ALL THE BOYS

Concepts in evolution

NT RLS LCTN

NH RTD TRTS

S PCT N

GN TCR CMB NTN

Concepts in evolution

NT RLS LCTN

NATURAL SELECTION

NH RTD TRTS

INHERITED TRAITS

S PCT N

SPECIATION

GN TCR CMB NTN

GENETIC RECOMBINATION

Tongue twisters

RDL RRY YL LWL RRY

SHS LL SSS HLL SNTH SS HR

PT RP PRP CKD PCKF PC KLD PPP R

HWM CHW DWLDW DCHC KCHCK

Tongue twisters

RDL RRY YL LWL RRY

RED LORRY, YELLOW LORRY

SHS LL SSS HLL SNTH SS HR

SHE SELLS SEA SHELLS ON THE SEA SHORE

PT RP PRP CKD PCKF PC KLD PPP R

PETER PIPER PICKED A PECK OF PICKLED PEPPER

HWM CHW DWLDW DCHC KCHCK

HOW MUCH WOOD WOULD A WOODCHUCK CHUCK

Represented by consecutive letters of the alphabet

JLN DKL VN

ST RNDB LGM

RN MND V NDM

FF TYN DNT HSND

Represented by consecutive letters of the alphabet

JLN DKL VN

JOULE AND KELVIN

ST RNDB LGM

AUSTRIA AND BELGIUM

RN MND V NDM

URANIUM AND VANADIUM

FF TYN DNT HSND

FIFTY AND ONE THOUSAND

They equal 42

FRT NTM STHR

TMC NMB RFM LYB DNM

SP TSNT WDC

LFT HNVR SNDV RYT HNG

They equal 42

FRT NTM STHR

FOURTEEN TIMES THREE

TMC NMB RFM LYB DNM

ATOMIC NUMBER OF MOLYBDENUM

SP TSNT WDC

SPOTS ON TWO DICE

LFT HNVR SNDV RYT HNG

LIFE, THE UNIVERSE AND EVERYTHING

Women involved in political scandals

MN DYR CDVS

DMS HRL YP RTR

MN CCG HLN

NTN DSN CH

Women involved in political scandals

MN DYR CDVS

MANDY RICE-DAVIES

DMS HRL YP RTR

DAME SHIRLEY PORTER

MN CCG HLN

MONICA COGHLAN

NTN DSN CH

ANTONIA DE SANCHA

These women made the headlines due to:

- Profumo affair
- Homes for votes
- Jeffrey Archer sex scandal
- Being David Mellor's mistress

Alan Partridge's format ideas

CKN GNP RSN

RMW RSTL NGWT HCH SND DV

NN RCTYS M

MN KYT NNS

Alan Partridge's format ideas

CKN GNP RSN

COOKING IN PRISON

RMW RSTL NGWT HCH SND DV

ARM WRESTLING WITH CHAS AND DAVE

NN RCTYS M

INNER-CITY SUMO

MN KYT NNS

MONKEY TENNIS

Pairs of homophones

CLN LNDK RNL

LL WDN DLD

QRN DC HR

SGH DND SD

Pairs of homophones

CLN LNDK RNL

COLONEL AND KERNEL

LL WDN DLD

ALLOWED AND ALOUD

QRN DC HR

QUIRE AND CHOIR

SGH DND SD

SIGHED AND SIDE

Proverbs about money

VR YMN HSH SPRC

FLND HSM NYRSN PRTD

RSNG TDLF TSL LBTS

THR SNS CHT HN GSF RLN CH

Proverbs about money

VR YMN HSH SPRC

EVERY MAN HAS HIS PRICE

FLND HSM NYRSN PRTD

A FOOL AND HIS MONEY ARE SOON PARTED

RSNG TDLF TSL LBTS

A RISING TIDE LIFTS ALL BOATS

THR SNS CHT HN GSF RLN CH

THERE'S NO SUCH THING AS A FREE LUNCH

Three consecutive numbers in ascending order

N NTN LVN

NN TY NNN HND RD NHN DRD NDN

MN SNZ RN

NN TNT WNT YTW NTYN

Three consecutive numbers in ascending order

N NTN LVN

NINE, TEN, ELEVEN

NN TY NNN HND RD NHN DRD NDN

NINETY-NINE, ONE HUNDRED, ONE HUNDRED AND ONE

MN SNZ RN

MINUS ONE, ZERO, ONE

NN TNT WNT YTW NTYN

NINETEEN, TWENTY, TWENTY-ONE

Same postcode district and US state abbreviation

DR BYN DD LWR

STL BNS NDL BM

PSL YND PN NSY LVN

LNC ST RND LSN

Same postcode district and US state abbreviation

DR BYN DD LWR

DERBY AND DELAWARE

STL BNS NDL BM

ST ALBANS AND ALABAMA

PSL YND PN NSY LVN

PAISLEY AND PENNSYLVANIA

LNC ST RND LSN

LANCASTER AND LOUISIANA

Punchlines

WH YTHL NGFC

TG TTT HTH RSD

NSH WN TFHR WNC CRD

NND TC RYTS NL YJK

Punchlines

WH YTHL NGFC

WHY THE LONG FACE?

TG TTT HTH RSD

TO GET TO THE OTHER SIDE

NSH WN TFHR WNC CRD

NO, SHE WENT OF HER OWN ACCORD

NND TC RYTS NL YJK

NO NEED TO CRY, IT'S ONLY A JOKE

The jokes with these punchlines are:

- A horse walks into a bar, and the bartender asks…
- Why did the chicken cross the road?
- My wife's gone to the Caribbean. Jamaica?
- Knock knock. Who's there? Boo. Boo who?

They begin with three vowels

LNHRP

DCLGN

JBRD

L

371

They begin with three vowels

LNHRP

AEOLIAN HARP

DCLGN

EAU DE COLOGNE

JBRD

OUIJA BOARD

L

AIOLI

Dickens quotations

LV RTW STHS SKD FRMR

TSF RF RB TTR TH NGT HTD

MTH GHS TFC HRST MSPST

NTT PTT FNPN TNT

Dickens quotations

LV RTW STHS SKD FRMR

OLIVER TWIST HAS ASKED FOR MORE

TSF RF RB TTR TH NGT HTD

IT IS A FAR, FAR BETTER THING THAT I DO

MTH GHS TFC HRST MSPST

I AM THE GHOST OF CHRISTMAS PAST

NTT PTT FNPN TNT

NOT TO PUT TOO FINE A POINT ON IT

These are quotations from:

- *Oliver Twist* (obviously)
- *A Tale of Two Cities*
- *A Christmas Carol*
- *Bleak House*

X and Y make Z

RDN DBLM KPR PL

SDM ND CH LRNMK SLT

RSR SNDT RDSM KSTRS

JH NN DDW RDM KJDW RD

X and Y make Z

RDN DBLM KPR PL

RED AND BLUE MAKE PURPLE

SDM ND CH LRNMK SLT

SODIUM AND CHLORINE MAKE SALT

RSR SNDT RDSM KSTRS

RISERS AND TREADS MAKE STAIRS

JH NN DDW RDM KJDW RD

JOHN AND EDWARD MAKE JEDWARD

Famous signoffs

GDN GHTC HLDRN VR YWHR

MYY RG DGW THY

DN THV NG HTMRS DSL PWLL

NDT SGD NG HTFRM HMG DNGHT

Famous signoffs

GDN GHTC HLDRN VR YWHR

GOODNIGHT CHILDREN, EVERYWHERE

MYY RG DGW THY

MAY YOUR GOD GO WITH YOU

DN THV NG HTMRS DSL PWLL

DON'T HAVE NIGHTMARES, DO SLEEP WELL

NDT SGD NG HTFRM HMG DNGHT

AND IT'S GOODNIGHT FROM HIM, GOODNIGHT!

These signoffs are associated with:

- *The Prisoner* (it's in the last line)
- Comedian Dave Allen
- Nick Ross on *Crimewatch*
- *The Two Ronnies*

Famous first lines from novels

THP STSF RGNC NTRY

HP PYFM LSR LLLK

TWST HDY MYG RND MT HRXP LDD

CL LMSH ML

Famous first lines from novels

THP STSF RGNC NTRY

THE PAST IS A FOREIGN COUNTRY

HP PYFM LSR LLLK

HAPPY FAMILIES ARE ALL ALIKE

TWST HDY MYG RND MT HRXP LDD

IT WAS THE DAY MY GRANDMOTHER EXPLODED

CL LMSH ML

CALL ME ISHMAEL

These are the first lines of:

- *The Go-Between* by L. P. Hartley
- *Anna Karenina* by Leo Tolstoy
- *The Crow Road* by Iain Banks
- *Moby-Dick* by Herman Melville

Complete: 'WHITE is to BLACK as ...'

CL NSTD RTY

SN WST CL

FR STSTS CND

BR RYST CLL

Complete: 'WHITE is to BLACK as ... '

CL NSTD TRY

CLEAN IS TO DIRTY

SN WST CL

SNOW IS TO COAL

FR STSTS CND

FIRST IS TO SECOND

BR RYST CLL

BARRY IS TO CILLA

Statistical terms

CNF DNCN TRVL

PSS NDST RBTN

NTRQ RTLR NG

RG RSS NLN

ANSWERS

Statistical terms

CNF DNCN TRVL

CONFIDENCE INTERVAL

PSS NDST RBTN

POISSON DISTRIBUTION

NTRQ RTLR NG

INTERQUARTILE RANGE

RG RSS NLN

REGRESSION LINE

Mnemonics

TH RTYD YSH THSP TMBR

BFRX CPTF TRC

VRYG DBYD SRV SFVR

RC HR DFY RKG VBTT LNVN

Mnemonics

TH RTYD YSH THSP TMBR

THIRTY DAYS HATH SEPTEMBER

BFRX CPTF TRC

I BEFORE E EXCEPT AFTER C

VRYG DBYD SRV SFVR

EVERY GOOD BOY DESERVES FAVOUR

RC HR DFY RKG VBTT LNVN

RICHARD OF YORK GAVE BATTLE IN VAIN

Famous newspaper headlines

DWY DFT STR MN

CRS SWH TCR SS

HLD NDL DND LD

FRD DST RRTM YHM STR

Famous newspaper headlines

DWY DFT STR MN

DEWEY DEFEATS TRUMAN

CRS SWH TCR SS

CRISIS, WHAT CRISIS?

HLD NDL DND LD

HE LIED AND LIED AND LIED

FRD DST RRTM YHM STR

FREDDIE STARR ATE MY HAMSTER

Twins

R NNN DR GG KRY

NT HNYN DPT RSH FFR

PLLN DR TMS

RB NND MR CGBB

Twins

R NNN DR GG KRY

RONNIE AND REGGIE KRAY

NT HNYN DPT RSH FFR

ANTHONY AND PETER SHAFFER

PLLN DR TMS

APOLLO AND ARTEMIS

RB NND MR CGBB

ROBIN AND MAURICE GIBB

Things that can be capped

L W L L

BN DWD TH

NGL SHCR CKTR

C NC LT X

Things that can be capped

L W L L

OIL WELL

BN DWD TH

BANDWIDTH

NGL SHCR CKTR

ENGLISH CRICKETER

C NC LT X

COUNCIL TAX

Party games

PNT HTL NTHD NKY

HN TTHT HMBL

LN DNB R DG

M SCL CH RS

ANSWERS

Party games

PNT HTL NTHD NKY

PIN THE TAIL ON THE DONKEY

HN TTHT HMBL

HUNT THE THIMBLE

LN DNB R DG

LONDON BRIDGE

M SCL CH RS

MUSICAL CHAIRS

Things a publican might say

TMG NTLM NPLS

PN TFT HSL

CND SLC

YRB RRD

Things a publican might say

TMG NTLM NPLS

TIME GENTLEMEN PLEASE

PN TFT HSL

PINT OF THE USUAL?

CND SLC

ICE AND A SLICE?

YRB RRD

YOU'RE BARRED

Days before English national bank holidays

STRS NDY

MN DYTH RSDY

N WYR SV

CH RS TMSDY

Days before English national bank holidays

STRS NDY

EASTER SUNDAY

MN DYTH RSDY

MAUNDY THURSDAY

N WYR SV

NEW YEAR'S EVE

CH RS TMSDY

CHRISTMAS DAY

End in _____ria

W STR

CFT R

R

PHR

End in ____ria

W STR

WISTERIA

CFT R

CAFETERIA

R

ARIA

PHR

EUPHORIA

Weather songs

TSR NNG MN

YRT HSN SHNF MYLF

RD RSNT HST RM

THW NDB NT HM YWN GS

Weather songs

TSR NNG MN

IT'S RAINING MEN

YRT HSN SHNF MYLF

YOU ARE THE SUNSHINE OF MY LIFE

RD RSNT HST RM

RIDERS ON THE STORM

THW NDB NT HM YWN GS

THE WIND BENEATH MY WINGS

Regional newspapers

DN BR GHV NNGN WS

STHW LSC H

STN GL NDL YTM S

WST RN MR NNGN WS

Regional newspapers

DN BR GHV NNGN WS

EDINBURGH EVENING NEWS

STHW LSC H

SOUTH WALES ECHO

STN GL NDL YTM S

EAST ANGLIAN DAILY TIMES

WST RN MR NNGN WS

WESTERN MORNING NEWS

Gender-swapped film titles

Q NKN G

THB YWT HTHD RGN TTT

LR DND THT RMP

TW LVNG RYW MN

Gender-swapped film titles

Q NKN G

QUEEN KONG

THB YWT HTHD RGN TTT

THE BOY WITH THE DRAGON TATTOO

LR DND THT RMP

LORD AND THE TRAMP

TW LVNG RYW MN

TWELVE ANGRY WOMEN

Orwellian 'characters' and the books they appear in

NP LNN DNM LFRM

BGB RTH RNDN NTNG HT YFR

GRGR WLLN DDW NNDT NPRSN DLNDN

GR DNC MSTC KNDK PTHS PDS TRFLY NG

Orwellian 'characters' and the books they appear in

NP LNN DNM LFRM

NAPOLEON AND ANIMAL FARM

BGB RTH RNDN NTNG HT YFR

BIG BROTHER AND NINETEEN EIGHTY-FOUR

GRGR WLLN DDW NNDT NPRSN DLNDN

GEORGE ORWELL AND DOWN AND OUT IN PARIS AND LONDON

GR DNC MSTC KNDK PTHS PDS TRFLY NG

GORDON COMSTOCK AND KEEP THE ASPIDISTRA FLYING

Two number one pop artists merged together

BYG RGM CHL

LT NJ HNL NNN

RYC HR LSZ NVR

CR GDV DB W

Two number one pop artists merged together

BYG RGM CHL

BOY GEORGE MICHAEL

LT NJ HNL NNN

ELTON JOHN LENNON

RYC HR LSZ NVR

RAY CHARLES AZNAVOUR

CR GDV DB W

CRAIG DAVID BOWIE

Famous Latin phrases from literature

CRP DM

DLCT DC RMST PRPT RMR

L CTS T

TM PRM RS

Famous Latin phrases from literature

CRP DM

CARPE DIEM

DLCT DC RMST PRPT RMR

DULCE ET DECORUM EST PRO PATRIA MORI

L CTS T

ALEA IACTA EST

TM PRM RS

O TEMPORA O MORES

These can be translated as:

- Seize the day.
- It is sweet and fitting to die for one's country.
- The die is cast.
- O the times! O the customs!

EastEnders Christmas storylines

PL NFW LRDS

DR TYD NH NDSN GDV RCP PRS

RN NMTC HLLS WPSB BY

KTN DLFL VLB RTS QR

EastEnders Christmas storylines

PL NFW LRDS

PAULINE FOWLER DIES

DR TYD NH NDSN GDV RCP PRS

DIRTY DEN HANDS ANGIE DIVORCE PAPERS

RN NMTC HLLS WPSB BY

RONNIE MITCHELL SWAPS BABY

KTN DLFL VLB RTS QR

KAT AND ALFIE LEAVE ALBERT SQUARE

A country and a landlocked part

NGLN DNDL CSTR SHR

TLY NDM BR

RP BLCF RL NDND LS

M XCN DC HHH

A country and a landlocked part

NGLN DNDL CSTR SHR

ENGLAND AND LEICESTERSHIRE

TLY NDM BR

ITALY AND UMBRIA

RP BLCF RL NDND LS

REPUBLIC OF IRELAND AND LAOIS

M XCN DC HHH

MEXICO AND CHIHUAHUA

World sport governing bodies and their sports

FFN DF TBLL

FN DTHL TCS

TTFN DTB LTN NS

FD NDC HSS

World sport governing bodies and their sports

FFN DF TBLL

FIFA AND FOOTBALL

FN DTHL TCS

IAAF AND ATHLETICS

TTFN DTB LTN NS

ITTF AND TABLE TENNIS

FD NDC HSS

FIDE AND CHESS

Descriptions of emojis

FCW THTR SFJY

DSP PNT DBTR LVDFC

RLLN GNTH FLR LGHN G

SM RKN GFC

Descriptions of emojis

FCW THTR SFJY

FACE WITH TEARS OF JOY

DSP PNT DBTR LVDFC

DISAPPOINTED BUT RELIEVED FACE

RLLN GNTH FLR LGHN G

ROLLING ON THE FLOOR LAUGHING

SM RKN GFC

SMIRKING FACE

Inventors and their inventions

CLTN DR VLVR

BRND BL LPNT PN

HR NBYN DMC CN

BY LSN DWN DPRD

Inventors and their inventions

CLTN DR VLVR

COLT AND REVOLVER

BRND BL LPNT PN

BIRO AND BALLPOINT PEN

HR NBYN DMC CN

HORNBY AND MECCANO

BY LSN DWN DPRD

BAYLIS AND WIND-UP RADIO

African countries with the first letter changed

MT HF RC

LG

BL

LN N

African countries with the first letter changed

MT HF RC

MOUTH AFRICA

LG

LOGO

BL

BALI

LN N

LENIN

If we restore the first letter we have:

- South Africa
- Togo
- Mali
- Benin

Only Connect question writers

VC TRCR NMT CHLL

RC HRDS MN

LNC NNR

DNLR DCL FF

Only Connect question writers

VC TRCR NMT CHLL

VICTORIA COREN MITCHELL

RC HRDS MN

RICHARD OSMAN

LNC NNR

ALAN CONNOR

DNLR DCL FF

DANIEL RADCLIFFE

AUDITION

Visit http://onlyconnect.online/audition to submit your answers.

5 points

Dennis Taylor (World Snooker champion)

3 points

Bon Scott (lead singer, AC/DC)

2 points

Ken Livingstone (Mayor of London)

1 point

Lincoln and Kennedy (US Presidents)

5 points

Epistle to the
Ephesians

3 points

The One Hundred
& Twenty Days
of Sodom

2 points

De Profundis

1 point

The Pilgrim's
Progress

5 points

England: Wales

3 points

Brazil: Scotland

2 points

Scotland: Trinidad and Tobago

1 point

Holland: Republic of Ireland

5 points

3 points

2 points

1 point

5 points

The Brittas Empire

3 points

Alice's Adventures in Wonderland

2 points

Vanilla Sky

1 point

Dallas (series 9)

5 points

Marathon

3 points

Hamburger

2 points

Alcoholic

1 point

Watergate

5 points

1st: Sighting

3 points

2nd: Physical evidence

2 points

3rd: Observation/ contact

?

5 points

$1 \rightarrow 8$

3 points

$8 \rightarrow 10$

2 points

$10 \rightarrow 19$

?

5 points

Tony Blair as PM
(Years 1–3)

3 points

Will Carling as
England captain
(Years 1–4)

2 points

John Major as PM
(Years 1–4)

?

5 points

3 points

2 points

?

5 points

Algeria = Algiers

3 points

Greece = Athens

2 points

Japan = Tokyo

?

5 points

Man

3 points

Protocol

2 points

Element

?

Ivory	Sooty	Bunyan	Grimes
Budd	Winklevoss	Kray	Paddington
Biffo	Glaucous	Wingrave	Iorek Byrnison
McWhirter	Red-billed	Herring	Baloo

King	En passant	Carney	Rockaby
Angel	Endgame	Storm	Leigh-Pemberton
Rogue	Footfalls	Happy Days	Gambit
Castle	George	Cyclops	Stalemate

Beard of the Year winners

JR MYCRB YN

G RTHM LN

RW NW LL MS

W W

Bond film titles, missing a word

RF RV R

L VN DD

DDY

F RMW THLV

Episodes of *The Jeremy Kyle Show*

LD TCT RSH CKRS

MYR CSTSS TRSS LSSM THR

TWF MLSTWR

HWC NBT HF THRW HNN VRV NSLP TW THY?

Punning hair-salon names

CTB V

SCS SRSS TRS

C RLPN DDY

JCKT HC LPPR

Acknowledgements

Jack, David and Victoria would like to thank:

The BBC, Ben Beech, David J. Bodycombe, Adam Bostock-Smith, Jeff Bowman, Chris Cadenne, Steve Castle, Rob Cawdery, Sarah Clay, Alan Connor, Hannah-Jane Davies, Janice Hadlow, Gilly Hall, Jon Harvey, Jenny Hawker, Llŷr Hughes, Rachel Hunter Hamilton, Peter Jamieson, Ben Jones, Siân G. Lloyd, Sara Low, Rhiannon Murphy, Daniel Peake, Shaun Pye, RDF, Huw Rees, Chris and Megan Stuart, Claire Tatham, Rob Thomas, Mike Turner, Alan Tyler, Howard Watson, Hywel Williams, Bethany Wright and all the crew in Cardiff, all the contestants who have ever come along to play, and all our wonderful question writers, in particular those not mentioned above whose questions appear in the book:

Christine Ansell, Olav Bjortomt, Andy Bodle, Jonathan Broad, Guy Campbell, Martha Casey, Travis Eberle, Kate Fenton, Jonathan and Rozann Gilbert, Tony Gold, Wei-Hwa Huang, Philip Marlow, Dave Mattingly, Chris Miller (CM), Chris Miller (KM), Alan Mortiboys, Tony Rubin, Hugh Rycroft, Justin Scroggie, Michelle Sinclair, Smylers, Ian Tullis, Laura Watson, Iain Weaver, Geraldine Wiley, Teri Wilson